Step Onto the Mat

Journey to True Success

Step Onto the Mat

Journey to True Success

Kevin Asano

WHITE
MOUNTAIN
CASTLE
PUBLISHING, LLC

www.whitemountaincastle.com

Step Onto the Mat
Journey to True Success

First Printing, August, 2008
Second Printing, August 2009

We want to hear from you.
Please send your comments or inquiries to:

White Mountain Castle Publishing, LLC
P.O. Box 700833
Kapolei, Hawaii 96709
Email: whitemountaincastle@yahoo.com
Website: whitemountaincastle.com

Scripture taken from the HOLY BIBLE, NEW INTERNATIONAL VERSION. Copyright © 1973, 1978, 1984 by International Bible Society. Used by permission of Zondervan Bible Publishers.

Published with permission from the United States Olympic Committee and the International Olympic Committee.

Edited by Dawn O'Brien & Elaine Terry
Text Design by Sherrie Dodo
Olympic Photos: David Finch/www.judophotos.com
Japanese Calligraphy of "Asano": Keisui Yoshii
Back Cover Photo by Marc Schechter

ISBN 978-0-9815219-1-6

Printed in China

This book is dedicated to my family:
To my wife Mari, my best friend and constant support,
And to my three beautiful daughters,
Rena, Anna, and Maya,
May this book inspire you to live a life that will glorify God.

Contents

Foreword

I first met Kevin Asano in 1978 at Grace Bible Church after a Sunday evening service. He was a rather smallish freshman on the Pearl City High School judo team and I remember praying with him. A week or so later, Kevin won the first of many national championships by defeating a stronger, more experienced competitor before a pleasantly stunned statewide television audience. It was his "coming out" moment.

In the media interview that followed, Kevin attributed the landmark win to his newfound relationship with God. It marked the beginning of an incredibly storied judo career that climaxed with the winning of the silver medal in the 1988 Olympics in Seoul, Korea. Kevin went far beyond most people's expectations. Except that Kevin is not "most people."

Kevin was deemed a long shot to succeed beyond high school competition. Experts said he was too small, too light, and too weak to step onto the mat and engage the "big boys," much less make the U.S. Olympic team. Therein lies the lesson from Kevin's life:

Put your trust in God
and never let anyone tell you that you can't do something until
you step onto your "mat,"
engage your opportunity, wrestle your opposition,
and give it your best shot.

Nearly 30 years later, Kevin continues to do just that. Parlaying the lessons learned in judo, his journey has taken him through a stint in the ministry as a pastor and now as a successful financial planner in the business world. More importantly, he is a family man, happily married to Mari and the doting father of three darling girls. And, yes, they too, have stepped onto the mat to learn lessons that far transcend the sport of judo.

SO WHAT ABOUT YOU?

What gift has God given you with which to bless others? What passion burns within you that when unleashed will add immense value to the lives of others? What are you waiting for?

Grab hold of the God who put you here, step onto the mat, and go for it!

Norman Nakanishi,
Senior Pastor, Grace Bible Church,
Pearl City, Hawaii

Introduction

This book began with a prompting and grew into an urging that wouldn't go away. As I discussed the wild-and-crazy idea of writing it with those close to me, I realized that I had a unique story to tell. This story goes beyond me and has the potential power to encourage anyone, even you, no matter what walk of life you come from.

You will quickly see that I am an ordinary man with many faults and shortcomings. Any glory should be reserved for the Lord Jesus Christ who has given me the sustaining strength to go beyond my personal limitations. I pray that this story gives you hope and inspiration to live your life in a way that will bring you true and lasting success.

*"Delight yourself in the LORD
and he will give you the desires of your heart."*

Psalm 37:4

*"Brothers, I do not consider myself yet to have taken hold of it.
But one thing I do:
Forgetting what is behind and straining toward what is ahead,
I press on toward the goal to win the prize
for which God has called me heavenward in Christ Jesus."*

Philippians 3:13-14

Prologue

On the morning of September 26, 1988, I stood on a bridge that overlooked the Olympic Village in Seoul, Korea. Most of the athletes were still in bed as the sun slowly came peeking through small patches of clouds and over the newly constructed high-rise buildings. The sound of birds singing in the crisp, cool morning air brought feelings of joy and wonder as I stood in my own quiet celebration.

Just the night before, I had competed in the extra-lightweight division judo finals in front of a worldwide audience. My quest for Olympic gold had ended, after losing to the Korean champion, but I was still thrilled and overwhelmed to stand on the winners' platform to receive the silver medal.

As I enjoyed the still ambience of the morning, I lowered my head over the railing and tears began to flow freely. Images from my eighteen-year journey to the Seoul Olympics flooded my mind. I saw myself as an excited seven-year-old boy eager to step onto the mat for the very first time. At nine years old, I saw myself win my first tournament and the Most Outstanding Player trophy that stood nearly three feet tall. I pictured my sensei's garage, where I spent many grueling hours training with my high school teammates. I remembered being victorious at national championships as a skinny, inexperienced freshman, and finishing off my high school career with my team winning the championships four years in a row.

Though the scenes held many successes, I also flashed through the hard times I faced: When my physical and emotional strength failed. When I was filled with so much discouragement and doubt that I wondered if I'd ever fulfill my goal of becoming an Olympian.

Yet each instance – whether glory or gory – came from the same source: God, who empowered me to pursue my destiny and complete the journey He had laid out for me.

This is my simple life story laid out like the framework of a house. Except that within the building of this house, breathed a living mystery of power beyond my person. And forged within was a giving treasure of lessons beyond anything I could claim to know. I reveal the mystery and the lessons both to you here.

ONE

The Journey Begins

There's a saying that good things come in small packages. Most babies look plump and healthy with rosy cheeks, but I came into this world looking like a skinny, wrinkled old man. Upon seeing me in the delivery room, my mom announced, "This can't be my son. Someone made a mistake!" At only six pounds and five ounces, I was a lightweight from the start.

I was born in Honolulu, Hawaii on April 20, 1963, to Henry and Karen Asano, third-generation Japanese Americans and parents for the first time. My parents were typical children of the 1940s and '50s. Like many of their peers in rural Oahu, their parents had worked hard on the sugar plantations. Determined to succeed in life, my dad volunteered for the Marine Corps. While serving his last year, he married his high school sweetheart, Karen Yoshikane.

Six months after I was born, our family moved to San Jose, California. Now with a family to support, he struggled through college while Mom worked full-time as a secretary at Lockheed. After graduating, he found a position working for the United States government in Okinawa.

JUST SUMMER FUN?

Our new town, which was located outside the United States military base, was full of wide-open spaces. What I liked best about living in Okinawa was my freedom. At the age of seven I was bursting with energy, and by the end of first grade Mom needed to find a summer activity that would keep me busy and out of trouble. What does a mother do with a boy who has boundless energy?

One morning as I waited across the street from our house for the school bus, my mom called out, "Kevin, would you like to take judo this summer?" I had no idea what judo was but it sounded like fun. "Yeah, I'll take judo," I yelled back. Little did I realize that this was the spark that would launch a lifelong journey. It was a chance encounter that would change the course of my life.

My summer was spent at the Kadena Judo Club on a United States military base. On the first day of practice, I was excited to see the other boys wrestling and couldn't wait to get onto the mat. As a beginner, I wasn't especially talented. In fact, I was one of the smallest, weakest players. Still, by the end of the summer, I was able to trade in my beginner's white belt for a yellow one. Rather than receive a brand new belt from my *sensei*, we had to hunt for a store in the open marketplace that sold yellow dye. Although you could buy a brand new yellow belt, the *sensei* probably thought I wouldn't continue judo, so this would be a cheaper, less permanent fast fix. However, in my little heart, that yellow belt was the greatest achievement in my seven years of life.

FIRST LESSON: HUMILITY & THE RUNT

Though the summer program ended, I was still excited about judo. My dad heard about a successful program at the U.S. Army Ryukyu Islands Judo Club, so he enrolled me there. My new teacher, Tsuruo Fukushima, was also from Hawaii. Fukushima *sensei* was in his mid-forties, a solidly built man with broad shoulders and kind eyes.

At first, I was a little intimidated by the size of the class, over 100 students. My only confidence came from my newly dyed, yellow belt tied around my waist. *Sensei* immediately stripped away my hard-earned yellow belt, demoting me back to a white belt. It was demoralizing, my first lesson in humility. Sometimes one has to take one step back before taking two steps forward.

Fukushima *sensei* was a strict disciplinarian. I had not quite mastered the technique of tying my belt into a square knot. When we lined up to bow after practice, he would call out, "Asano, come here." *Sensei* would untie my belt, then retie it the correct way and rap me on the head with his knuckles for me to remember. The pain lasted for a moment, but I loved having *Sensei*'s undivided attention in front of the entire class.

Sensei wisely toughened us up. When a student cried because he stubbed his finger, *Sensei* inspected it to make sure it wasn't serious and then said, "You still have nine other good fingers!" He knew when a child was faking it and when it was real. Most of the time, our pride was hurt more than our bodies. With the older boys he was strict and harsh, but with us his actions displayed care and love more than anything else.

As the runt of my class, my peers usually got the best of me. But I was also a scrapper, ready to go with anyone even if I typically ended up on my back. I liked the challenge. Seeing my initiative, *Sensei* encouraged my dad to keep bringing me back.

MY DAD'S BEST MOVE

Dad was usually the one who took me to practice and that thirty-minute drive became "our time." He often told me stories about forest animals and their fun-filled adventures. Sometimes the stories were so funny that he would laugh too; years later I found out his stories were made up on the spot.

When we discussed my judo he always showered me with positive affirmation. Because of my fighting spirit, he nicknamed me Tiger, and even stopped using my real name. I complained, "Stop calling me Tiger. It's embarrassing!" I sulked, thinking *What if my friends hear him?* Yet by calling me Tiger, my father was building my confidence; I began to believe that I was fierce enough to take anyone on the mat.

FINDING MY ROAR

It took awhile before I could actually prove my ferocity in tournaments. In the first few competitions, when I won a match, I would sit straight with my head held high like a champion. When I lost, I dejectedly hung my head as tears welled in my eyes. It felt like the end of the world.

It took me months to finally win my first trophy. In the final match for a championship, Doug, a fellow teammate who was a head taller and twenty pounds heavier, demolished me. I settled for first runner-up, but it became the new highlight of my life. My heart swelled as I showed the high school boys my great achievement. Even my dad made a fuss, taking it to the local trophy shop to have my name engraved on the nameplate. When we went to pick it up, I was a little discouraged to find that my eight-inch trophy was puny compared to the others. But the disappointment faded as I walked out, my new trophy a gleaming symbol of success.

MY GREATEST FANS

Although Dad and Mom were my greatest fans, they approached the tournaments in different ways. Dad, the silent type, was always in the background, never saying much until the match was over.

Mom, on the other hand, yelled at the top of her lungs. Even with over 500 cheering fans, I could still hear my mom's *"Come on,*

Kev!" As embarrassing as it was, it felt good to have someone on my side. Mom was also there to absorb my nervousness. She was the one who got pre-tournament headaches, stomachaches, and butterflies. With her love and support, how could I possibly lose?

Where Dad and Mom were my frontline supporters, my younger siblings, Gary and Michelle, were my silent cheerleaders. They had no choice but to tag along to every tournament and special event. Although I stepped onto the mat alone, my whole family was with me.

STEPPING ONTO *YOUR* MAT

After all these years, I can still see myself in front of Fukushima sensei. His attention told me that he cared for and believed in me. And I can still hear my dad calling me Tiger because he saw my potential. Both men started me on a lifelong journey of judo that has since impacted all aspects of my life.

Who are the people in your life that have played an important role in nudging you along on your life's journey?

If you are older, who are the people in your life that you are intentionally working with to make a lasting impact in their lives?

TWO

Seeds of Greatness

After only one year of judo, my dad was transferred back to Hawaii. My first priority was to find a judo club. Fukushima *sensei* suggested the Pearl City Judo Club. When I visited, I knew right away that I wanted to join. Practices were run by two teachers: Yasuyuki Sakabe *sensei* and Yotoku Maeshiro *sensei*. Sakabe *sensei*, originally from Japan, was the all-Navy champion and a strict disciplinarian. On the other hand, Maeshiro *sensei* had a gentleness that made the students feel loved. He instilled in his students respect, discipline, and confidence. The club offered a good balance of inner growth and athletic competition.

There were more than two hundred students at that time, so we never lacked for partners. In fact, there was so much competition that we held inner-club tournaments. I made it to the finals at my first club competition and was matched against a kid who was thirty pounds heavier. By sheer size and power, he crushed me. I got up crying, not because of the physical pain but because I wanted to win so badly.

SWITCHING SIDES

As a youngster my dad participated in judo and karate. This practical foundation along with his keen analysis gave him the ability to dissect my matches and provide tips that gave me the competitive advantage to win. For example, since most players were right-handed like me, he quickly encouraged me to become left-handed. He knew I would be comfortable against the right-handers yet they would be uncomfortable with my left-handed grip. Since I was only nine years old, I could easily change.

At first I didn't want to switch because I didn't want anyone to beat me while I got accustomed to the new grip. It was awkward and frustrating. But my dad's insight paid off: after six months of training, I was strong and confident on my left side and began beating opponents. This one tip instantly advanced my judo to a higher level.

STREET FIGHTING & GETTING IT RIGHT

Using judo to win at tournaments was one thing and using it to beat up others was another. Judo should never be used as a weapon to cause trouble, and our instructors constantly instilled in us that we were taught to avoid conflict. Instead of listening, I chose to learn self-control the hard way. I believed I was invincible.

In the fifth grade, I entered a local tournament where I recognized an older, blond-haired boy from my elementary school. I easily won my division and saw that he didn't even place. When we got back to school, I decided to pick a fight, thinking I could beat him up. Although he was at least six inches taller and twenty pounds heavier, I knew I was stronger. After all, I was a winner and he was a loser.

We agreed to rumble after school. The final bell became our ringside bell and we faced off, staring each other down. After sizing each other up, he said, "Come on, let's do it!" His first punch landed like a battering ram in my gut. I immediately keeled over in pain and staggered back, trying to recover. I couldn't breathe. I couldn't stand upright. I couldn't think straight. A moment later, a second right landed in my gut, and I fell to the ground writhing in pain. That humiliation became a life lesson in humility: judo is for tournaments, not the streets.

INJURIES OFF THE MAT

Other challenges threatened to floor me outside of judo. From the time I was a baby, I suffered skin rashes and allergies. As a young boy, I felt self-conscious about my rash, the small patches covering my hands, arms, and legs. It itched and I couldn't help but scratch. At times it got so bad that the skin on my right hand cracked and oozed. My parents tried all kinds of remedies, from traditional medicine to unconventional treatments. None helped.

I always wondered why I had to put up with a constant itch and rash. Perhaps it enabled me to have a higher pain tolerance. I could push my body harder and longer, and it helped me make greater gains in my training regimen. When my physical body reached its limit, my mind would take over and push my body further. I knew what it was like to experience daily, nagging discomfort so I never took my physical health and ability for granted.

With all of the physical contact in judo, I never received a major injury from the sport. Instead, my injuries came off the mat.

LOSING OLYMPIC MEDAL, DISCOVERING OLYMPIC DREAM

My first serious injury may have come in the fifth grade while waiting at a bus stop, but little did I realize that it was a premonition for my Olympic run. I was on my way to see the movie *The Three Musketeers*. As I waited, I saw a storm drain with a large metal grill covering. And as I stared at the bottom of the drain, I saw what looked like a Japanese coin. Instantly I was struck with an illogical and terrifying thought: *Is that my commemorative coin from the 1964 Tokyo Olympic Games?*

Just before going to the bus stop, I had sat in my room admiring my Olympic coin that my favorite aunty had given me. One side depicted Mount Fuji—special to me because of my Japanese ancestry. The other side showed the Olympic rings—my first tangible connection to the Olympic Games. Gazing at the coin in my room, I had thought, *Wouldn't it be great to compete at the Olympics!* This coin became a seed of my Olympic dream. I had carefully rewrapped the coin in tissue paper and put it back in my drawer before running off for fun at the movies.

It was impossible that the coin at the bottom of the drain was my Olympic coin, but in my temporary insanity, I feared the worst. I stuck my left hand into the metal grill and lifted the cover. The grill was so heavy that, as I strained to lift and move it to the side, it smashed and fractured my hand. With a deep groan I struggled to free my hand from its weight. I went into semi-shock when I saw my hand was already swollen to twice its size. Undeterred, I scampered down the drain with one hand to retrieve my precious coin. I discovered a one-yen coin made of aluminum.

Instead of enjoying the movies that day I went to the doctor's office to get a cast. That yen cost much more than a pretty penny. But more importantly, that fracture left a bump on my left hand that, to this day, still reminds me of my first encounter with my Olympic dream.

GETTING UP CLOSE TO AN OLYMPIAN

Successful judo players were heroes and role models to me. At the 1976 Montreal Olympic Games, United States heavyweight Alan Coage won a bronze medal. I was so proud to see a United States judo player featured on television. This was only the second time a U.S. judo player had won an Olympic medal.

On Coage's team was another great player, Patrick Burris. One of his parents was originally from Hawaii and a few months prior to the Olympics, Burris stopped by our judo club to practice. To a thirteen year old, Burris was a superstar bigger than life. I marveled at his judo – a mix of grace and power. He was the first Olympian I had ever met and I wished to be like him one day. It was another step toward my dream and destiny.

LIGHTING THE TORCH

The summer after the 1976 Olympics, my dad said something that became a defining moment in my life.

As he drove me to judo practice one afternoon, he turned and said matter-of-factly, *"Kevin, one day you can be the first judo player from the United States to win a gold medal at the Olympics."*

Without looking at him, I continued to gaze at the cars on the freeway. Something inside clicked as I processed every word. *Does Dad really believe that I can go to the Olympics? And win a gold medal? If my dad believes in me, maybe it's possible.* That day my dad planted seeds of greatness in my heart. And with the passing of each day, those seeds began to take root, sprout, and slowly grow.

EYE OF THE TIGER

In the eighth grade, judo took on a more prevalent role in my life. No one had to push me; I had developed a passion to excel. Now, more than ever, I wanted to win and was willing to train and sacrifice to become the best. Right before I began high school, I competed in a state high school tournament and won my division. In my very first attempt, I had made it to the top of Hawaii high school judo. Next I set my sights on the national championship.

STEPPING ONTO *YOUR* MAT

The importance of having a vision for your future is vital. My dad planted in my young heart the dream of winning Olympic gold; I eventually made it my own. That vision helped me to focus and stay committed.

There have been times in life when I didn't have a significant dream. Looking back I've noticed that during these times I felt lost and lacked motivation and purpose. However, the larger my dream, the more excited I am about life. My challenge now is to keep my dreams big and not settle for mediocrity.

What is your dream?
If it doesn't scare or excite you, perhaps, it isn't big enough.

THREE

Beyond Judo

When I got a special transfer to start at Pearl City High School, a school known for its judo program, I thought it was to further my judo career. However, that move impacted my future in another significant way.

Because I was new and didn't have many friends, I started hanging around the juniors I met in band class. One of the guys invited me to a youth rally. That evening, more than one hundred young people from various high schools came together. The speaker shared the importance of having a personal relationship with Jesus Christ. As I listened, I realized something in my life was missing. Up until that evening, I had thought everything was going pretty well and never thought I needed God. I realized an emptiness in my heart that could only be filled by God; no amount of accomplishments, accolades or friendships could fill it.

At that moment I knew that I needed a personal relationship with Jesus Christ. With trembling hands, I prayed and invited Jesus Christ into my life to become my Lord and Savior. I asked Him to forgive me of all the wrong and shameful things I had committed and I asked Him to help me live a life that would be pleasing to Him. I felt an overwhelming peace come over me. I knew I had made the right decision.

A MENTOR

A few weeks later, Lance Sokugawa, a judo player from my club who was seven years older than me, invited me to Grace Bible Church. There I reaffirmed my faith in Christ. Initially there was no obvious external change but, over the weeks, I noticed my desires for personal glory and recognition begin to fade. Instead, my focus was to live a life that would glorify God. Amazingly, my passion for judo increased and I became more motivated to excel in judo.

Every Sunday, Lance took me to church. Then he would buy me dinner, saying, "When you get a job, you can treat me." Lance was my mentor and hero, both as a judo athlete and as a Christian. He was the top extra-lightweight judo player in Hawaii and was also nationally ranked in the top five. His body was chiseled from intense training; to me he looked like Mr. Universe. Lance had perfected his throws and could literally dump larger opponents. Every time he competed, the audience waited for a spectacular throw. They were rarely disappointed. Though fierce in competition, he was humble and friendly off the mat.

COACHES & MORE COACHES

Throughout my high school judo career, I was fortunate to have some of the most caring and diligent mentors and instructors. Larry Iwamuro was our team trainer. Iwamuro *sensei* had retired from the Army and devoted most of his time and energy to training us. He had started judo as an adult student of Fukushima *sensei*, my knuckles-on-the-head teacher back in Okinawa, so their methods were similar. They both focused on the fundamentals of judo and implemented strength and conditioning methods like no one else in the country.

Iwamuro *sensei's* house was a regular site for training. The whole team, almost twenty boys, spent the first forty-five minutes cramped in his living room doing homework. He believed smart students made strong competitors. After that, we would get down to the business of training—warming up with three hundred push-ups, one hundred sit-ups, and other torturous exercises on his front lawn. It was funny to see the new boys struggling to keep up with the push-ups for the first time. One boy couldn't bend his arms to comb his hair or brush his teeth for days. We laughed when we heard that, a cheerful respite from otherwise painful afternoons.

Once we were fully fatigued from warm-ups, Iwamuro *sensei* would bring us into his homemade torture chamber, which doubled as his garage. In this chamber we pulled on bicycle inner tubes attached to the wall to strengthen our arms. For leg sweeping strength, we pushed five-gallon plastic buckets filled with rocks and sand across the garage floor one hundred times with each leg. For speed, we did side sweeps on automobile tires as hard and fast as we could, again one hundred repetitions on each leg, while our partner stood on the tire to keep it in place.

For stamina, we ran up and down the steeply sloped street, sometimes with leg weights strapped to our ankles. *Sensei* would watch eagle-eyed from the sidewalk. To improve our throwing, he employed one of his most brutal tactics: A student was strapped to a padded cushion using inner tube tires and then his partner was to attempt lifting and throw him. A primitive form of interisland flight? I've yet to figure it out. Regardless, Iwamuro *sensei* stood there making sure we gave our best effort and correcting every little mistake. After the torture chamber, we would head to practice at the club, again greeted by Iwamuro *sensei*.

Since training in his garage was like being in hell, my teammates affectionately nicknamed him "The Devil." Even two hundred-plus-pound heavyweights became meek and mild when face-to-face with Iwamuro *sensei*'s five-foot-seven, 140-pound frame. Just one look from his steely eyes would melt the toughest player.

OF *SENSEI* & SENSIBILITY

In 1976, my old teacher Fukushima *sensei* retired from his federal job in Okinawa and moved to Hawaii to coach alongside Iwamuro *sensei*. Now we were doubly blessed – not only "The Devil" himself but also his mentor. In reality, these two men were angels sent by God. They devoted their time and energy because they believed in us and wanted us to succeed. When I felt like breaking down they always seemed to know to ease off. They forged my foundation in judo.

I thrived on pain and often challenged my body beyond its physical limits. I made sure that I did every push-up and during the last ten repetitions I pushed to finish off with twenty. When we ran, I always tried to finish first. No matter what the exercise, I tried to outdo everyone else. I knew that with every day of intense training, I was one step closer to realizing my dream.

BREAKING THROUGH

Judo challenged me beyond my limits. When I stepped out on the mat, the competition was between my opponent and me. Winning and losing provided instant feedback on my progress. My parents never pushed me; I wanted to win so I pushed myself. No matter how hard the practice, I always wanted to be there.

Iwamuro *sensei*'s attendance policy was that you had to be dead or dying to miss practice. He believed that if you injured one arm, you could still use your good arm. If you couldn't work out at all, you could still learn from the sidelines. No one had the guts to ask *Sensei* to be excused from practice.

Two older teammates, Glen Watanabe and Steven Nohara, were in my weight class. Every day we pushed and pounded each other. We fed off each other's intensity and practice often turned into all-out battles. I always got an adrenaline rush practicing my throws with Steve. With each set of throws, the harder I slammed him to the mat, the harder he slammed me. The great thing about judo is that, because we knew how to fall properly, we could blast each other with all our might and still not sustain an injury.

Our team was like a fraternity of brothers that trained together for a common goal and in the process also developed lifelong friendships.

DISCIPLINED DIET?

Despite the strict training regimen, we never followed a strict diet. I regularly treated myself to a large cheeseburger, a fried fish sandwich and a large order of French fries at the local fast food place. To keep costs down and fool myself into thinking I was eating healthy, I ordered water instead of soda.

One diet tip I did pick up from one of my *sensei* was to eat garlic and tofu before tournaments. I wasn't sure of any scientific reason but I didn't bother to question him. So before every tournament, I cringingly ate cloves of garlic lightly sautéed with a few drops of shoyu. (I could handle the garlic but never the tofu.) Although the garlic wiped out my taste buds, I always seemed to do well the next day. It probably had more to do with my overpowering breath and body odor.

When the judo season began that spring, our team was hungry to dominate the league. We had trained hard and sacrificed so much that we weren't going to let anyone get in our way. We easily won the championship and took home a lion's share of gold and other medals in the individual championships. Finally we understood why our *sensei* had pushed us so hard.

GOING TO NATIONALS

To mentally prepare for competition, I spent hours picturing myself defeating each of my opponents at the high school nationals and standing triumphantly on the winners' platform. Those images kept me on course when training was difficult or when I felt physically overwhelmed. Once in awhile, running up and down Iwamuro *sensei*'s street, I secretly hoped a car would run me over so I could rest. The only thing that kept me going was my vision of winning and giving all the glory to the Lord.

As a freshman, I entered the national high school competition against the best in the country knowing that winning was a lofty dream. On the day of competition, I whispered a prayer to God and asked for strength. I promised that I would give Him the glory no matter what happened. I battled through my bracket and made it to the final round. My opponent was an experienced Los Angeles senior, an accomplished wrestler who could bench-press over twice his weight and had to lose ten pounds just to make weight. I was an inexperienced kid. The match was broadcast on local TV and even the commentator remarked that I didn't have much of a chance.

Throughout the match I strained to keep up. My opponent used his experience to thwart all of my techniques. In the last minute, I received a warning from the referee for noncombativity. I thought I had received a penalty not realizing it was only a verbal warning. Thinking I had nothing to lose, I threw myself into the match. When the final buzzer sounded, the two side judges both awarded me the win. I was stunned.

When I stood on the winners' platform to receive the gold, I had a big smile and lifted my hand to make the number one sign. I was pointing to heaven, saying, "Lord, You are number one and deserve all the glory."

STEPPING ONTO *YOUR* MAT

When competition is keen, confidence can make the difference between winning and losing. Before a match, I had to condition my mind to push aside doubts and fear and instead step forward with confidence to achieve my goal. I knew tournaments were won or lost before the actual competition. My success came from training physically, emotionally, mentally, and spiritually.

Hard work is like investing for the future. If you prepare well, you will have the confidence to seize your goals.

Do you have the confidence to succeed?
If not, what changes do you need to make now?

FOUR

Too Tired to Cry

Winning was contagious and I wanted more. After taking the gold at the high school national championships, I wanted to rise to the next level. So I trained hard my sophomore year and was ready to compete at nationals the following May.

In my semifinal match, I faced a tough *judoka* from Massachusetts. I threw him backward with an *ouchi gari* (major inner reaping throw). He fell back on his butt and I landed forward on my knees and between his legs. I clearly scored but the referee awarded him the point. I ended up losing the match. I was upset and disappointed. This was the first time I had lost a match by a referee's mistake.

That loss taught me three things: First, even referees make mistakes. Second, I needed to win decisively and eliminate any possible confusion. Third, I learned humility. I had become proud and saw myself as bigger than I really was. This loss kept me humble.

JUDO IN JAPAN

That summer, Iwamuro *sensei* took five other students and myself to Japan to improve our judo. He told us that we were going to "eat and sleep judo" every day for two months. I was excited to train in Japan, confident that I would do well since I was one of the best high school lightweights in the U.S.A.

We trained in Kumamoto, a southern prefecture, at Kyushu Gakuin, one of the top judo high schools in the nation. Coach Reisuke Shiraishi was the former instructor of Japan's judo superstar, Yasuhiro Yamashita. As a college student, Yamashita had won the most coveted title in Japan, the All-Japan Championships. He would eventually go on to win nine consecutive All-Japan Championships, four World Championships and an Olympic title. He was undoubtedly one of the finest and most famous players in the history of judo. Athletes from all over the world sought Shiraishi *sensei*'s expertise. He was highly selective, so it was a great honor and privilege to train with him.

GOING AGAINST JAPAN'S BEST

I quickly got my first taste of world-caliber judo. One of Shiraishi *sensei*'s former students, Kenichi Haraguchi, visited. Haraguchi was the top university student in the extra-lightweight division, which happened to be mine. Shiraishi *sensei* paired the two of us together for a fifteen-minute workout.

I couldn't believe the level of judo Haraguchi displayed. He was the meanest, fastest, and strongest judo player I had ever trained with. He choked and arm-locked me into submission with techniques I had never seen. He slammed me flat on my back with a combination throw that was so fast and hard it knocked the wind out of me. With each new move, he flashed me a sly smirk. It became obvious he enjoyed seeing me wince though he politely apologized whenever he saw I was in pain. He also took time to teach me some of my most valued judo techniques. This gave me a clear gauge of where I stood in relationship to the world's top extra-lightweight competitors—nowhere!

TRAINING JAPANESE STYLE

It became apparent that our six-day training regimen back in Hawaii paled in comparison to the Japanese style. Not only did they train six days a week, often twice a day, but many of the top schools arranged for their athletes to live together year round in a dorm and under the watchful eye of their coaches. For them, there was no way to cut out from practice. Judo wasn't just a major part of their lives; it *was* their life! The level of dedication, discipline, and intensity these student-athletes devoted was unbelievable.

Many of the stronger players would go on to major in physical education at college; additionally, their future careers were based on the sport. It was no wonder Japan had the best program in the world. If I wanted to take my judo to the international level, I would have to train as hard and intensely as the Japanese.

TURNING UP THE HEAT

That summer in Japan was hot, humid, and humiliating. The instant we stepped outside, we began to sweat profusely. All of a sudden Iwamuro *sensei*'s garage seemed like paradise compared to our new "hell." We practiced for four hours a day, six days a week, sometimes twice a day. The lightest Japanese judo player in the forty-member team was more than fifty pounds heavier than my 115-pound frame. Everyone easily beat me during those two months.

One day I was so drained that I crumpled in the corner, looked out the window, and tried to cry. The tears wouldn't flow. I had no energy left to push the tears out.

I did, however, have several moments of victory in Japan, with three events when I clearly clobbered my Hawaii teammates. The first was when we had a rice-eating contest at dinner and I downed ten bowls of rice. The second was eating the most watermelon… though my teammates didn't know that I ran back to my room to vomit the seedy contents and felt sick for the rest of the night. The third clear-cut victory came when I stood ankle-deep in an icy cold river the longest. Otherwise, I had no victories that summer. It was another huge helping of humility.

HALFWAY HOME

Halfway through our Japan trip, my five teammates and I went out to lunch at a nearby ramen shop. A table calendar reminded us that it was only July and we still had one more month of training. We were beaten up, tired, and homesick. It was not turning out to be the exciting trip we had hoped it would be. Deep inside, I thrived on the training; I knew it would pay off once we got back to Hawaii. Shiraishi *sensei*'s training that summer left an indelible mark on my judo career.

Upon returning home to Hawaii, we started practice the very next evening. I was surprised at my speed, strength, and technique. Everyone else seemed to be moving in slow motion. My confidence level skyrocketed. The hard work and sacrifice had paid off and I knew that the next two years of high school competition would be my best.

STEPPING ONTO *YOUR* MAT

In Japan, I faced judo players with world-class talent. I thought my dedication to judo was strong. Two months in Japan helped me to gain perspective, develop character, and keep me on track with greater goals.

When I allow pride and overconfidence to seep into my heart, I inevitably set myself up for a fall. I constantly deal with my self-centeredness.

Having good character is like building a strong foundation. We all know successful men and women who, because of poor character, faced financial collapse, broken relationships, or personal devastation.

What areas of character do you struggle with?
If you want to be a champion, start strengthening your character.

FIVE

A Better Plan

Before summer's end, I went on a much-anticipated, five-day summer youth camp. Many of the students had gone the year before and had discovered a new love for God and a passion to serve Him. I had to be there!

At the camp, I had a vivid dream. Five words flashed through my mind: *"You are a chosen generation."*

I had never seen those words before and wondered where they came from. The next morning the camp speaker opened his Bible and read that exact phrase and went on to explain it. He revealed that God has a plan for our lives: *To declare the glory of God to the world.*

By the end of the week I was totally on fire. I wanted to live my life fully for God and make a difference in the world. I was willing to do anything and go anywhere, even if that meant becoming a missionary in a remote part of the world. At the same time, my passion and excitement for judo had evaporated.

I could no longer see the advantage of doing judo in light of a greater calling to serve God. If I wanted to do ministry, I couldn't waste time! I decided to quit judo, transfer to a Christian high school, and devote all of my energy to ministry. In my zeal I was convinced this was the right thing to do.

PERSUADING EVERYONE ELSE

I went home and shared my new plan with my parents and *sensei*. They could not believe such a radical turnabout in only one week. Though they did not agree, my parents supported me. I took the entrance exam for the Christian school and was ready to dive in.

The following week, my dad went to Iwamuro *sensei* to discuss my decision. They talked for some time before my dad asked me to join them. "Kevin, I don't usually tell you what to do," my dad started, so I knew it was serious, "but in this situation do what I tell you. You need to go back to judo at Pearl City High School. You won't understand why I'm making you do this, but when you're older you will."

I burst into tears. I couldn't believe what I was hearing. Once I regained my composure, I told my dad, "I don't agree and I don't understand. But the Bible says that I am to obey you. I will obey your word." Then, with no emotion, I added, "I'll do judo until I graduate from high school. Once my obligation is fulfilled, I will quit judo."

WHY, GOD?!

I was devastated. I couldn't believe it was God's will for me to return to judo. How could it be? I was willing to give up everything. What greater sacrifice could God desire?

The next morning, I drove to Pearl City High School to reregister for school. On the way home, I shared with a friend the pain and confusion I was going through. At that moment a song came on the Christian radio station that was an answer to my question. It encouraged me to wait on the Lord and learn the lessons He wanted to teach me. In His timing, God would reveal what He had in store for me. I still didn't understand but my heart said it was right.

Later, it became obvious that I needed to discern God's will and purpose from my emotions and feelings. Something inside of me changed. Judo took on a greater purpose: It was my direct assignment from God. He was directing my destiny.

The next two years brought tremendous success. Our high school team again won the team championships. I won two more national championships, was undefeated by any high school opponent, and won outstanding competitor awards locally and nationally. Through it all, I gave the glory to God.

HORSING AROUND

As a senior, I was a captain on the judo team and it was my responsibility to lead and motivate the team by example. Unbeknownst to me, my teammates sometimes complained to our coaches that I pinched them in practice. The coaches never caught me doing it, but if they had confronted me, I would have told him that I never pinched. Instead I gave them a "horse bite." The difference between a pinch and a "horse bite" is that a pinch only uses two fingers but a "bite" uses the whole hand.

It was my way of 'motivating' my teammates and it worked especially well when the guy was pinned and wouldn't try to escape. This, however, was not as effective as my ultimate motivation tactic. When a teammate simply wouldn't move, I kissed his sweaty cheek. As you can imagine, he went ballistic and escaped my pin. In my defense, I did it only a few selected times and never made it a habit.

GOOD NEWS & NOT QUITTING

During my senior year I also helped establish a Bible study on campus. That initial ministry became the seed for hundreds of many future high school students to hear the good news of Jesus Christ.

Later, I discovered that one of the youth pastors had heard I had wanted to quit judo and attend a Christian school. He also thought it was the wrong decision (though he didn't express his feelings at the time), knowing I would have a greater impact for God by continuing judo at Pearl City High School.

I thought my greatest impact as a Christian would be to leave everything and become a missionary in a foreign country. God's plan was better. And I had only started to see the first phase of His plan... the rest was yet to be unveiled.

STEPPING ONTO *YOUR* MAT

When my dad told me to go back to judo, I didn't understand. My misconception was that truly dedicated Christians became pastors or missionaries. I didn't see judo as a special gift God had given me.

I've come to realize that the best way to serve God is in the unique way He has called me. When I was younger it was as a student-athlete. Now it is as a judo sensei in the community and as a businessman in the marketplace. Every day I look for opportunities to reach out and help others in need.

What do you feel is your calling and vocation?
How can you best impact your world to help others?

SIX

What Do I Have to Lose?

At the end of my senior year, my coaches and teammates wondered if I would be voted Athlete of the Year. To their disappointment— one I tried not to share—a football player won. However, Coach Leigh was able to recognize me as the Outstanding Judo Player of the Year. During his allotted time at the microphone he shared my accomplishments and boldly proclaimed that I would one day represent the United States at the Olympic Games. It was flattering but I had to wonder if he was mistaken.

HANGING IT UP

After graduation, I had fulfilled my commitment to my dad and to God so I hung up my judo *gi* and called it quits. I had enjoyed a wonderful career but I was burnt out – too many years of rigorous and disciplined training. I had given up much of my free time for judo and I just wanted to relax and enjoy the things I never had time for before. The truth was that I didn't have the passion to compete at the next level, though I was considered a top judo player in the nation. Other than going to college, I didn't know what I wanted to do. The only thing I was sure about was that I did *not* want to do judo.

I enrolled at the University of Hawaii in the fall of 1981 with no major. First I considered premedicine but I just couldn't get excited about chemical symbols or microorganisms. Next I thought about engineering but calculus was too abstract. I couldn't grasp the concept of derivatives even when the professor tried to relate it to drinking beer. By the end of my first year, I was still searching.

College was so different from the disciplined routine of daily judo. I only had to study. With my newfound freedom, my commitment to Jesus Christ began to wane. At first it was subtle. Then, as the weeks and months went by, my heart moved farther and farther away from God. Of course I continued to attend church and Christian functions, appearing to be a dedicated and happy Christian. After all I knew the right things to say and do. Yet on the inside, I was drifting. Despite my internal conflict, I stubbornly continued my wayward course.

A COMEBACK

Though I was firm in my intention to never compete in judo again, God had other plans. One of Hawaii's major judo associations – the 50th State Judo Association – was chosen to host the U.S. Junior National Championships in 1982. Albert Aoki *sensei*, the chairman of the association, was the major key to bringing this tournament to Hawaii for the first time. The tournament would showcase the best seventeen- through twenty-year-old players in the country. It reignited my Olympic dream, and I was curious to see how I would do at this new level.

"What do you have to lose?" I pondered. "You don't have to spend any money to travel and this is a great opportunity to see if you have what it takes for the Olympics." With one part hope and an equal part of self-doubt, I made a deal with God: If I placed in the top three, I would consider vying for the 1984 Olympic team.

The crazy part was that I hadn't trained for one year and this elite event was only a month away! It would take a miracle. I quickly devised a "crash training" schedule to get my body back into its former shape. In such a short time, all I could do was sharpen whatever skills I had and hope for the best. I was realistic about my chances: My only hope was to take out my opponent in the first minute, before exhaustion set in.

1982 JUNIOR NATIONAL CHAMPIONSHIPS

The day of competition finally arrived and my stomach churned with butterflies. Fukushima *sensei* devised my game plan: "Kevin, you'll have to throw your opponent off the grip," he advised. "Before he gets a chance to grab your *gi* (uniform), beat him to the punch, grab his *gi* and throw him. Catch him off guard and he won't know what hit him."

It worked! My opponent and I bowed, took several steps toward each other and then I grabbed him and pounded him with a beautiful *ouchi gari* (major inner reaping throw). The match was over. The strategy worked for the next two matches, with a total combined time of less than thirty seconds for all three wins. My escape plan was simple and effective: Instead of "stop, drop, and roll," my version was "start, grab, and throw!"

SEMIFINALS & FINALS

My semifinal match was against a top player from San Jose State University. San Jose State's judo program and its head coach Yosh Uchida were equally legendary. Under Coach Uchida's direction, their team had won nineteen out of twenty collegiate national championships. In the United States, they were the best, bar none.

I faced Uchida *sensei's* star player. I was intimidated, having seen him destroy his competition in the preliminaries and knew he was eager to do the same with me. As we stepped onto the mat, I glared into his eyes and prepared for a battle. The referee shouted, "*Hajime!*" Immediately, my opponent aggressively came for me but was careful not to let me get a grip. After several seconds of fighting, my rival shot his favorite throw, *uchimata* (inner thigh throw). Instinctively, I sidestepped his hurling body and countered with a *tai otoshi* (body drop throw) for an *ippon* (full point)! Before either of us knew what was happening, he was on his back and the match was over. The crowd roared as their hometown boy toppled the San Jose State giant.

My final match lasted the longest at ninety seconds and I won the gold medal. Who would have imagined a win at junior nationals after one month of training? And to cap it off, I received the tournament award for Most Outstanding Competitor. How was this possible? Was it a miracle?

STEPPING ONTO *YOUR* MAT

I always marvel at how God opens doors of opportunity that change the course of our lives. When Aoki sensei brought the junior nationals to Hawaii, it drew me back to judo. When Fukushima sensei gave me that last-minute game plan, I won in a spectacular way. I never duplicated this feat in my whole judo career.

When I trust God, He nudges me toward my destiny. I don't have to worry about the future or try to make things happen on my own. He is there to guide me and help orchestrate the outcome. It is liberating to know that God is in control and will guide and direct my path. My responsibility is to discern His leading and, by faith, step through the doors of opportunity.

What doors of opportunity have you walked through that have had positive results?
What doors of opportunity are open to you now?

SEVEN

Heart of a Tiger

Up to this point the Olympics had been a fantasy; now it was a new horizon. Still, it was also a long shot. A very long shot. Top contenders for the 1984 team had already been competing at the senior level for at least four years. With the Olympics only two years away, I hoped to make the team with no prior experience. I had a choice: To either pursue my dream or continue on the same easy path.

I prayed, "God, I want to make the right decision and I need Your guidance." So heavily did this weigh on my heart that I decided to fast and pray for three days. During that time, I took a piece of notepaper and drew a line down the middle to list the pros and cons.

As I prayed and pondered my decision, I realized my only obstacle was fear: Fear of failure and of the unknown. Everyone – including my parents, instructors, and pastors – urged me to go for it. A new passion and purpose surged through me by the end of the third day. I decided to go for it and take the greatest risk yet.

CONFIRMATION FROM GOD

Soon after, a senior member of the church told me about an incident that had happened a few weeks earlier. He had been driving in Honolulu by the Neal Blaisdell Center when he had a strong urge from the Holy Spirit to stop and go inside. He had no idea why but he obeyed. He noticed there was a judo tournament happening that day and when he walked in, he saw me competing.

He came to understand that he was to let me know that God was orchestrating the outcome. This validated my decision: God was confirming that I was indeed moving to my destiny.

However, there were still people in the Hawaii and United States judo communities who didn't believe it. They felt I was too small, too weak, too young, and too inexperienced for the Olympics. In many ways they were right. Coach Leigh told me I was a little too young to be a 1984 Olympian, predicting it would more likely happen in 1988. I couldn't imagine training for another six years; I was set on 1984 or nothing.

FIRST SENIOR COMPETITION

Three months later, I got my first taste of senior competition at the U.S. Open. This was an event where international players were invited to compete at the Olympic Training Center in Colorado Springs, Colorado. It was one of two tournaments used to qualify for the Olympic trials. Because I dominated my divisions in high school and had won the junior nationals, I anticipated a respectable showing.

In my first match I faced Edward Liddie, top ranked in the United States and the top contender for the Olympic team. Ed was four years my senior and several inches taller, so he had to fight to stay under the weight limit. Adrenaline coursed madly throughout my body and my heart pounded a crazy beat as I stepped up to face him. As we got into the thick of our match, I was able to hold my own, until Ed came in for a *kani-basami* (flying scissors) that caught my left ankle. Despite the sharp pain, I continued to battle but couldn't keep up the intensity. Ed's ability, strength, and experience proved too much and he won by a unanimous decision.

This shattered any idea I had entertained of making an impact at the senior level. If I really wanted to prepare for the intense and heated competition of the Olympics then I would have to go through extreme and focused training. I needed to go to Japan.

HOW CAN I GO?

Thanks to a couple of high-level recommendations, I was accepted to train at Tokai University. At the time, Tokai had one of the best university judo teams in Japan, meaning it had one of the strongest teams in the world. Only a select few were admitted onto the team on a long-term basis and I was fortunate to make the cut.

To get psyched for my journey, some friends took me to see *Rocky III*. The theme song, Survivor's "Eye of the Tiger," made me flash back to the early days when my dad called me Tiger. Twelve years later, it was time for this Tiger to fight for his Olympic dream. Nothing was going to stop me.

Ready for Japan, my next dilemma was a nagging question, "How am I going to pay for this?" My parents weren't rich and they certainly couldn't afford the $20,000 it would take for a year in Japan. I was surprised when my dad and mom approached me and said, "Kev, we believe in you. Whatever it takes, we'll get the money." They knew that if God's plan was to have me train for the 1984 Olympics, then He would provide. He did.

STEPPING ONTO *YOUR* MAT

Training in Japan required a big commitment. No one could make the decision for me; the motivation had to come from within. I took the risk and went. From that point on, I did whatever it took to live my dream and make the Olympic team.

Over the years I've met other athletes who shared the same dream. As it turns out, many never made the journey because they never made the initial commitment.

You can have the loftiest dream, the best intentions and even the most detailed ideas to do great things in life, but unless you make the commitment to do it, nothing will ever happen.

What is stopping you from making the commitment
to start your dream's journey?
What will it take for you to make the commitment?

EIGHT

Onegaishimasu (Please)

The day of my departure arrived, Sunday, February 13, 1983. On the plane, I was apprehensive about the journey ahead yet excited about my new adventure. I was nineteen years old and it was the first time I was traveling to a foreign country alone. I didn't have the comfort and security of a coach, teammates, or my family.

When the plane landed at Haneda Airport in Tokyo, I didn't know who would meet me. As I emerged from customs, two huge judo athletes greeted me with my name on a sign, just like a tourist. As they escorted me to the van, we tried our best to bridge the communication gap – me in my broken Japanese and they with their limited English. Our conversation didn't go very far and I settled down for the three-hour drive to the university.

It was hard to believe that I was in Japan pursuing my Olympic dream! It was my first time in Tokyo and I marveled at the buildings, landscape, and traffic. After awhile, I drifted off to sleep in the back seat. The next thing I knew, the driver hit an abrupt stop at the university. I rolled off the seat and fell to the floor with a thud. The guys in the front seat chuckled. This was prophetic of my next two years.

When I got off the floor, I noticed that we were surrounded by rice fields. Tokai University was far removed from big-city life. At least, I reasoned, there wouldn't be any distraction from training.

ARRIVING AT TOKAI JUDO

My teammates dropped me off at the International Residence, the dormitory for foreign guests. Yoshio Matsunaga *sensei* was there to meet me and I was relieved to hear him speak fluent English. Then I met Keiko Mitsumoto, the manager of the dormitory, who also spoke English. I didn't feel as lonely and secluded anymore.

Matsunaga *sensei* helped me get settled and gave me a practice schedule. The next morning I would go to the *dojo*, meet the *sensei,* and watch the team practice. My training would start in the afternoon with a fifty-minute run. It was hard to sleep that night; I could hardly wait to meet my teammates and begin training.

The first thing that caught my attention when I arrived at the *dojo* was the enormity of the structure. The building was designed in traditional Japanese style with high ceilings; it loomed larger than life, more of a temple than a sports facility. Everyone removed their shoes before entering, the same tradition as when one entered a home in Japan. The floors of the entry and hallway were covered with dark wood panels in classic Japanese decor. This huge building was divided into two sections: the left side held the *kendo dojo* and the right side housed the *judo dojo*. Each could easily accommodate one hundred athletes. The changing rooms, showers, weight room, wrestling room, and boxing ring were located in the basement.

MAKING A CHAMPION

Matsunaga *sensei* then introduced me to Tokai University's head judo coach, Nobuyuki Sato. My first impression was one of a dynamic and charismatic leader. Sato *sensei* was one of Japan's top coaches. At six feet and 210 pounds, he was a former All-Japan and World Champion who still worked out with the collegiates, commanding respect with his superior skill. Whenever he stepped onto the mat, the atmosphere of the room changed and practices became more intense.

"Kevin, welcome to Tokai University," Sato *sensei* said in English. "I have been looking forward to meeting you. Aoki *sensei* told me you want to go to the Olympics. I will do my best to make you into a champion."

I knew this was not an empty promise. Sato *sensei* produced many of Japan's national and international champions. At the same time, many of the top foreign competitors and even Olympic gold medalists sought Sato *sensei*'s expertise. They often trained at Tokai.

Matsunaga *sensei* then introduced me to the rest of the teaching staff: Hideharu Shirase *sensei*, Yasuhiro Yamashita *sensei*, Hidetoshi Nakanishi *sensei*, and Kenichi Haraguchi *sensei*. Then I met the judo team. There were about eighty black belts, all bigger than me. I was 128 pounds; the average player was 175 pounds and the largest athlete weighed more than 360 pounds. Even the lightweights were heavier!

Already intimidated, I became even more uncomfortable when Sato *sensei* introduced me: "This is Kevin Asano from Hawaii. He is a U.S. Junior National Champion here to train for the U.S. Olympic Team. Take good care and work out hard with him." I felt like a target. It was like an open invitation for his boys to see how strong this American champion really was. I tried to brush aside my feelings and regain composure. These guys were tough but I thought I could hold my own. I'd show them how we do judo in Hawaii.

A FAMILIAR FACE

Later that afternoon Haraguchi *sensei* met me at the International Residence. We had met four years earlier; now he was contending for a spot on the Japanese Olympic team. It was good to see a familiar face and he immediately put me at ease with a friendly welcome. Apparently he remembered all the beatings he had given me.

We met up with about fifteen lightweights. Although I had never enjoyed running, my competitiveness always drove me to finish at the front of the pack. At this first session, I wanted to show them that I was no slouch. We jogged to a building with a ten-story, spiral staircase. For the next thirty minutes we went up and down the building: running, hopping on one leg, running backwards, and piggybacking a partner. After the run we did push-ups, sit-ups, and other strengthening exercises for twenty more minutes. I felt I had given a good first impression. This wasn't going to be as hard as I had previously imagined.

WITH EACH DRUM BEAT, A BEATING

The next morning practice started at 9:30 sharp with *randori* (sparring). We were scheduled for sixteen rounds, six minutes each, which was double what I was used to. Suzuki was the first to run up to me, bow and say, "*Onegaishimasu*" ("Please allow me to work out with you"). What he probably thought, though, was, "Please allow me to give you a thrashing." Within thirty seconds he threw me flat on my back. I quickly got up and doubled my efforts but Suzuki threw me just as quickly, only with a different throw. I tried harder but was thrown again. After six minutes of pounding by Suzuki, the time keeper beat the large *taiko* drum at the far left corner and shouted, "*Nihon me!*" or, "Round two!" Suzuki bowed and said, "*Arigato gozaimasu*," or, "Thank you very much." I heard it as, "Thank you for building my self-esteem as I tossed you all over the mat."

Another lightweight named Yamashita ran up and said, "*Onegaishimasu*." With Olympian intensity, he immediately slammed me into the mat full force. Next were Konno, Ono and Hamano—each opponent tossed me like a bag of rice, and I landed on my back every time. Each beat of the drum brought a new line up of eager opponents, vying to take me on. Practice had turned into a mini-tournament to test the Hawaii champion. It didn't take long to realize that I was no threat. In fact, I was turning out to be a pretty good practice dummy.

BEAT AT MY OWN GAME

Before going to sleep that night I wondered what went wrong. I had never been beaten so badly in my weight class. After all, I was a high school and junior national champion. I was thoroughly humiliated by these Japanese players. I consoled myself by thinking, *Don't worry Kevin, you'll show them tomorrow. They beat you standing, but your forte is really newaza (matwork consisting of pins, chokes, and arm-locks).* I couldn't wait to redeem myself.

The next day, Hamano was the first to greet me with his sly, *"Onegaishimasu."* In less than a minute, I was on my back with my head wedged between his rib cage and left arm, squirming to get out of his pin. Next up, Tanaka said, *"Onegaishimasu"*—"Please go with me, so that I can get you into one of my painful arm-locks." Then Inoue invited me, *"Onegaishimasu"*—"Please work out with me, so I can choke you out cold." As each guy had their turn, they seemed happy to beat me in the matwork a.k.a. up-close-and-personal human torture. Later I found out that Tokai had one of the toughest *newaza* teams in the country. In fact, Sato *sensei's* nickname was *"Newaza* Sato."

Not only did I lack in judo skills, I also suffered in strength and stamina. In the weight room, I was the team's weakest man. They always had to take the weights off for me. I couldn't understand how after years of training under Iwamuro *sensei*, I was still so weak. I felt like a flea among giants.

GETTING WORSE

During long distance runs, the gap grew greater. The slowest student had to wait so I wouldn't get lost running through the town and rice fields. I knew Olympic training would be difficult, but I didn't realize how far I had to go. Dreams of storming Japan with my superb skills quickly evaporated.

This was the hardest training I had ever encountered. To my Japanese peers, this training was easier than high school training. I became even more determined.

Several times each year we had intense one-week training camps. These were especially hard during summer and winter's extreme conditions. August's heat and humidity made regular life in Japan uncomfortable. Add to that training in a building with no breeze and wearing a thick judo *gi*, it became unbearable. Water became a precious resource guzzled during breaks. Over the course of a single practice, I easily lost five pounds of water weight. Because I was from Hawaii, I somehow handled the summer training. On the other hand, nothing prepared me for winter camp.

We started practice at five in the freezing morning. I would go to bed with my judo *gi* on for two excellent reasons: I didn't have a heater and I didn't want to have to change the next morning. Wake up was at 4:30 A.M. in order to make the twenty-minute trek to practice. There the coaches opened the windows to allow in the icy fresh air. The cold mats made my bare feet feel like they were burning on ice. The only way to warm up was to work out hard, and on those mornings, everyone worked out extra hard.

The *sensei* said this was to strengthen our determination and resolve. They must really have believed it because they had to wake up and get out of bed as early as the students. While I struggled to keep up, the team took it as par for the course. Yet deep down I knew I was training with the best athletes in the world. The larger the reward at the end, the more difficult the journey to get there.

BEYOND THE DOJO

Once I settled into the daily routine, I began looking for a church. One of my pastors in Hawaii told me about Elmer Inafuku, a Hawaii missionary who was now a pastor in Tokyo. The one hour and ten minute train ride from Tokai to Shinjuku was well worth the commute; I felt instantly at home with this new spiritual family. On my first visit I mentioned that I hoped to see Tokyo's cherry blossoms. Without hesitation, a new friend took me to Ueno Park to see hundreds of cherry blossom trees in full bloom.

Pastor Elmer proved to be a successful role model. He had grown up in Hawaii but felt called to pioneer a church in Tokyo. Nearly twenty years later, he had a beautiful wife and four wonderful children, spoke fluent Japanese, and had a dynamic church. In Japan, where Christians comprise less than one percent of the general population, Pastor Elmer's church was a mega-church with 200 members. His willingness to follow God's lead and commit his life to full-time missionary work had impacted countless people. One day I wanted to be just like him.

BACK IN THE U.S.

After two months of intense training in Japan, I returned to the United States to enter the U.S. Senior Nationals in Los Angeles. This was crucial because it offered one of two chances to earn points to qualify for the Olympic trials; as yet I had no points. Points were based on how one placed: First place received five points, second place received three points, and third place received two points. The five athletes with the highest point totals were then invited to compete at the Olympic trials. Though my Japanese teammates were still pounding me daily, I thought competition against Americans would be easier in comparison. My mom flew to Los Angeles to cheer me on and together we celebrated my twentieth birthday. I was determined to take home a gold medal as my birthday present.

In the second round of competition I faced Roy Nakamura. His style seemed awkward, which I interpreted as a lack of skill. I entered the match with too much confidence and was soundly defeated! I continued in the losers' bracket and faced a competitor from San Jose State University.

Less than a year earlier, it had taken me only thirty seconds to beat their star at the junior nationals. I thought this competitor would be no match to my superior talent. Again, I was wrong. I left the tournament without a medal or any Olympic trial points. The only thing I took back was a bruised ego and a large dose of humility. I returned to Japan with renewed determination.

STEPPING ONTO *YOUR* MAT

The first day of practice in Japan was an eye opener. I knew I was in over my head and would have a long and tough road to success. If I wanted to win, I needed to focus and make judo my priority.

I've had several chapters in life when I had to start from the bottom. With a strong will and determination, I focus my energies to reach my goal. Remember, there are many good things in life, but they can be an enemy to what is best.

What do you have in your life that may be preventing you from focusing on what is best?

NINE

Never Say Die

When I returned to Tokai University, Sato *sensei* moved me to an off-campus dorm with nine teammates. He wanted to give me a real Japanese judo athlete's lifestyle, as too much comfort wasn't toughening me up. The International Residence was a clean, new facility with air conditioning, heating, individual kitchens and showers in each room, and even security guards. In contrast, Yoshimiso was a traditional Japanese-style boarding house. My room was a small *tatami* room (approximately ten feet by ten feet) with no amenities. I appreciated my new room and the landlords, the Aokis, who took care of us and made me feel at home.

Each building had a common kitchen. The bathroom was simply a toilet basin over a large hole in the ground where you had to squat to do your business. This turned out to be a great training for judo as I strengthened my legs. Even in the privacy of my bathroom, I was straining and training!

There was no sewer system; a truck, called a "vacuum car," would come to suck up all the waste from the hole. I quickly learned how to breathe with my mouth instead of my nose. My fear was that something important, like my wallet, would fall into the hole, and I would never want to retrieve it. Or, worse yet, something would crawl out of the pit and bite me.

The bath was another surprise. In traditional Japanese bathing, one washes the body first, then steps into the tub for a relaxing soak. Not at our boarding house. After practice, every one of my nine sweaty dorm mates would jump into the tub and wash later. Grit and grime filled the water, new attackers for my practice-weary body.

SUFFERING THE SEASONS

As an initiation, a new dorm mate helped me shave off all of my hair. This turned out to be a blessing in the hot season. Though I had lived in Hawaii nothing could prepare me for the Japanese summer. There was no breeze in my room and I refused to buy a fan. I was trying to save the forty dollars.

That same mentality prevented me from buying a heater when winter came. For a boy from Hawaii, freezing cold translates to the low sixties. It dropped into the thirties. The only warmth in my room came from my electric blanket and a *kotatsu*, a low Japanese table with a heater underneath. I spent most of my time snuggled in the blanket or under the *kotatsu*. I could see my own breath even in my room.

The good part about being at Yoshimiso was that our meals were prepared. We dined at a local *shokudo* (dining hall) where Mr. Masakatsu Kurakake and his wife prepared delicious meals that always included a bowl of rice, miso soup, pickled vegetables, and a main dish. The first Japanese phrase my teammates taught me to say was *"okawari onegaishimasu"* for an extra bowl of rice.

WHEN IN JAPAN, SPEAK JAPANESE!

Like most *yonsei* (fourth-generation Japanese-Americans in Hawaii), I could barely speak Japanese; and most of my teammates at Tokai couldn't speak English. If I wanted to ask them to stop beating me so mercilessly, I would have to learn Japanese. I enrolled in an intensive Japanese language program at the university. Class was seven hours each weekday and three hours on Saturdays.

After a grueling judo workout I would study for three to four hours, yet still couldn't grasp the language. It was frustrating not being able to communicate at practice and being left out of conversations. I wanted to learn Japanese almost as much as I wanted to make the Olympic team.

Japanese, like many languages, has different styles of speaking. There is the proper way that the language teachers espouse, and the colloquial way that locals speak. Japanese athletes also have their own lingo. For example, among judo players the word omae is used for "you" when speaking to a peer or underclassman. I heard it every day, so I naturally used it with others. When I called a girl at my church by saying omae for "you," she was appalled. She told me never to use that word in public as it was very rude. I joked with my judo friends that I picked up all of their low-class and no-class language.

In Japanese, sometimes the literal meaning doesn't match up. Take for example the meaning of judo, "the gentle way." Much of my judo experience was anything but gentle. I took beatings that left bruises, cuts, sprains, lumps, aches and pains. I would probably rename judo "the brutal way."

DISCIPLINE & RESPECT THE HARD WAY

Discipline and respect are very important in judo, principles I once saw driven into the head of a student. Literally! While practicing with another university judo team, the *sensei* was explaining something but the student continued to talk with a friend. With a quick snap of the wrist, the *sensei* used a bamboo stick to whack him on his head. The crack brought silence. Seconds ticked away as eternities with the student cradling his head and gritting his teeth in pain. The message was clear: Respect *sensei* at all times.

Another time at this same university, a student was fooling around when a *sensei* decided to teach him a lesson. He grabbed the student, went to the mat and applied a choke. The student immediately tapped out, signaling surrender. Instead, the *sensei* held the choke until the student passed out. The *sensei* immediately let go but when the student regained consciousness, they started again. The *sensei* choked out the student three times. Everyone watched, no doubt feeling sorry while some felt he deserved it. You would think I learned from watching others suffer. Not so. I chose to learn the hard way.

At the same club while waiting for practice to begin, I looked over and saw a senior heavyweight – over six feet tall and 260 pounds – lying on the mat. He looked like a beached whale. I knew him casually so I laughingly told him about his resemblance, calling him *debu* ("Fat pig!").

Instantly he pinned me to the mat, jumped on my back, and choked me from behind. Normally I would've tapped out, but the image of the other student being choked out three times flashed in my mind. I saw myself sprawled out on the mat, unconscious, while the rest of the team laughed. So I fought for my life.

For the next fifteen minutes the senior tried to slip his hand under my neck to choke me out. Indeed, the other students watched in amusement, enjoying the sight of their man teaching a puny *gaijin* (foreigner) a lesson. Finally the *taiko* drum sounded for practice to begin and he left me stunned, lying on the mat and shaking inside. The only reason he wasn't able to choke me out was because his hand was bigger than my head; he couldn't fit it under my neck!

DEVELOPING AN ATTITUDE

Judo, like in any sport, takes on a different mindset in elite training for championships. My goal was to make the Olympic team and compete against the best in the world for a medal. This required total sacrifice with a "never say die" attitude.

After taking daily beatings with little improvement, the only player I beat was a freshman smaller than myself. And a few girls! How could I compete with the world's best? These thoughts weighed me down and if I didn't snap out of it, I would eventually self-destruct. I decided to focus on developing a mental toughness along with my physical training. I knew winning wasn't based solely on ability or talents but on the will to win and a positive attitude.

With every beating I took, I resolved that it would make me stronger. I kept reminding myself that the first year is the most difficult and would tell myself, "Hang tough, Kevin. You can do it!" I *believed* that I would eventually be a winner.

That was a tough challenge in the face of daily beatings. For example, Daiya Sekimizu, a former high school national champion was now a student in my weight division and could throw me with every throw in the book. When I first worked out with him as a college freshman, I couldn't believe his mastery. He would come at me with total abandon and thrash me mercilessly. On the occasion when I actually gave him a challenge, he would extend practice from the standard six minutes to twelve or eighteen. He always got the best of me! Competition aside, he was a kind friend and instrumental in improving my judo. Despite the daily beatings, I enjoyed our workouts. And with every fall, I knew was getting better.

Another student who beat me daily and befriended me was Makoto Tanaka. When we first met he thought I was polite and had a childlike cute face. After our first *randori* session, he also found out that I was weak. Every day he threw me around and worked me over like a rag doll. He also took time after practice to teach me two of his favorite techniques—*tomoe nage* (circle throw) and *juji-gatame* (cross arm-lock)—which became my favorite techniques.

Whenever I felt like giving up, I reminded myself of my vision and why I was in Japan. If God gave me the desire to be there, He would give me the grace and strength to be successful eventually.

The Lord was using one of the best judo programs in the world to sharpen my judo skills, despite appearances to the contrary.

A positive side of hard training came in appreciating life's simpler comforts. During the hot summer, water from the faucet became a cool and refreshing drink that quenched my thirst like nothing else. The monotony of food choices became delicious to my famished body. A hot shower without a showerhead became a relaxing massage that washed away my sweat and body aches. And at the end of the long days, sleep came easily as I dreamed of Olympic glory.

PRACTICE BY PRACTICE, PERFECTION

Each practice taken alone was bearable. If we trained every other day, my body could recover and be ready for the next practice. That was not the case. Normally it was six afternoons a week of judo for three hours. Add to that four mornings a week of weight lifting or running. It was mentally challenging to be ready so often. Some days I felt like I was dragging myself to the *dojo*. It didn't make things any better when my *gi* was still damp from the previous workout. Especially in cold winter months!

The daily, weekly, and monthly grind made training brutal. I always seemed to be nursing some kind of injury. When one injury healed, another took its place. Probably the most painful bruise was to my tailbone; that forced me to sit out for nearly a week. At other times foot sweeps struck sensitive shins. I improvised and wore soccer shin guards to bear the brunt of the agony.

Regardless of how I felt before practice, once we bowed in and warmed up, it was all business. I left all the excuses and negative thoughts at the door and walked in with the intensity of a champion.

NO PRACTICE? STILL PRACTICE!

Whenever an injury sidelined me from judo, I would lift weights instead. It was during one of these rare occasions that I made one of my greatest strides. The downstairs gym contained wrestling mats and a wrestling dummy. At that time, I was struggling to perfect my *tomoe nage*, a sacrifice throw where you roll onto your back, place your foot on your opponent's stomach, and throw him over your head. When I tried it on the dummy, which weighed eighty pounds, it slipped and landed on top of me. Even the dummy gave me a hard time!

My execution was sloppy and I couldn't control the dummy for a clean throw. Either it slipped and landed on me, on its head, or awkwardly on the mat in the wrong position. Even if everyone else was beating me, I wasn't going to let a dummy beat me.

Over the next few days I went back to the dummy. I scrutinized my every move. Finally I worked out the kinks and consistently slammed the dummy square on its back. I was ready for a real opponent. The next day, I threw some of the guys with my *tomoe nage*. In fact, it became my favorite throw, one I became known for in the judo world. All because of an injury that forced me to stop training and allowed me to focus on improving. And yes, thanks to a dummy!

AWARD-WINNING TEAM

One of the goals of the Tokai judo team was to win the crown jewel of competition, the All-Japan University Team Championships. Each university selected their seven best players, regardless of weight, and competed regionally to qualify. When our team won, it gave me my first taste of being part of an elite-level championship team.

That year also proved to be a great year for Tokai University at the 1983 World Championships in Moscow. Haraguchi *sensei* lost a close match and placed third. Nakanishi and Yamashita *sensei* dominated their divisions and won the gold. Being on a winning team helped to boost my confidence in the midst of my personal struggles, and I was reassured that I was training with a championship team.

MIRACLES FED MY DREAMS

While I struggled to fulfill my dream, my family struggled too. Every time I needed more money to keep going, my mom would miraculously make a real estate sale. God's timing was simply amazing. Thanks to my parents and my siblings making tremendous sacrifices, my training was truly a family effort.

With tight finances, God got creative in paying my bills. For instance, He blessed me with Katsunori Kudo, a generous friend who owned a popular sushi restaurant. Every so often, he invited me to an expensive dinner of sushi and gourmet dishes, without charge.

COMPETING FOR OLYMPIC TRIALS...AGAIN

In the fall of 1983, I again entered the U.S. Open at the Olympic Training Center. At the same tournament a year before, I had lost my first match to Ed Liddie. This year I made it to the semifinals, where I faced a tough Korean. I was no match to his power. After losing, I faced a top-ranked player from the U.S. It was a grueling match but I won by a split decision. All of my hard work had paid off: I had finally broken into the United States national ranking!

However, I quickly discovered that I was still short on points and ranked seventh. Only the top five players were invited to the Olympic trials. From hopeful and encouraged, I became devastated and discouraged. After all of my effort, I still wasn't qualified. I had failed to make the 1984 Olympic trials.

With this discouraging news, I began to reassess. I could easily return to Hawaii; I had done my best and was never going to make it to the Olympics. Giving up was my first instinct. But not yet; I couldn't leave Japan as a failure. Neither my judo nor my fluency in

Japanese was satisfactory. Even if I didn't reach my original goal, I decided that I would still leave a champion! Thus I began my second year in Japan with a renewed vision.

SPRING 1984
NEW CLASS, NEW NAME & NEW HOPE

In the spring of 1984, a new freshmen class joined our team. I was respected as a second-year upperclassman. Instead of just "Asano," I had become "Asano sempai." It was strange to hear as most of the freshmen were bigger and stronger than me.

With the inflow of new faces came an influx of new hope penetrating the gray clouds of my first year's defeat. Occasionally I would have a magical day where I could beat the same guys who treated me like a rag doll a year before. I wasn't the weakest anymore and I began to lift as much weight as the others. Even during runs, I sometimes ended up at the front half of the pack instead of lagging way behind.

I completed my one-year intensive Japanese course and was accepted as a freshman student at Tokai University. After struggling for a year, I was able to engage in meaningful conversations with my teammates. Every day at practice my friends still beat me up but now I knew they cared and wanted to see my judo rise to the next level.

ENDING MY 1984 HOPES

That summer, the U.S. National Judo Team invited me to train in Argentina and compete at the Pan American Championships in Mexico City. This was the first time I traveled outside of Japan and the United States to do judo. I enjoyed the festive city of Buenos Aires and being in a country where people spoke only Spanish. During my entire trip I managed to learn only one Spanish word: *agua* (water). In Mexico City, I witnessed extreme poverty and wealth and had the thrill of climbing up the great Pyramid of the Sun, the largest Teotihuacán Aztec pyramid. I met players from many of the Pan American countries and gained valuable international competitive experience. I lost to a tough Brazilian but came in third place.

Still, I hadn't realized my dream of competing at the 1984 Olympic Games. I began to wonder if I wanted to pay the price for the next four years to compete at the Seoul Olympics in 1988. For my final six months in Japan, my future was unsure.

FUN IN THE LAND OF THE RISING SUN

Even with the demanding schedule of judo and school, I was still able to enjoy other activities and new experiences. During the last several months, I took on several jobs teaching conversational English. I also enjoyed the college group at the Shalom Church in Shinjuku. Though Sunday was my only day to recuperate, being in the presence of God and fellowshipping with Christians helped me to trust the Lord for my strength. I loved to play music and performed with a church band.

Before Christmas, I said my final goodbyes to the many people who had supported me during my stay in Japan: my judo *sensei* and teammates, my Japanese language class, the community families and my church. The two short years (though they seemed much longer) were full of experiences both wonderful and difficult. My judo went from a junior national level to a senior international level. I had matured as a person.

The 1984 Los Angeles Olympics had come and gone, and people asked about my future plans. Would I compete for the 1988 Seoul Olympics? After all, I was only twenty-one years old; my competitive prime was still to come. The United States judo organization had high hopes for me but I was mentally and emotionally drained. I couldn't see myself committing another four years of sacrifice and hard work just to have my dreams dashed again. To those who asked, my response was the same: "I've given up judo for good."

Little did I realize how mistaken I was.

STEPPING ONTO *YOUR* MAT

In life I come across difficult situations where I feel like giving up and wonder if it is worth the effort. In these times I step back and reevaluate what I'm doing and why I am doing it. Once I determine what I'm supposed to do, I push through until I find the breakthrough point. Sometimes it takes days, sometimes years. In either case, I make a conscious decision never to give up.

Too many people give up too soon and never find the breakthrough they hoped for. If you want success, you need to struggle and fight to get it. Nothing of great worth in life comes easily. The greater the dream is, the steeper and harder the climb.

What mountains are you facing today?
How will you overcome these?
What are the breakthrough points to anticipate?

TEN

No Regrets

Christmas was a wonderful homecoming in Hawaii with my family. I planned to finish school at the University of Hawaii, find a good job, get married and live a content, normal life. Deep down inside, however, I couldn't suppress the Olympic dream. For six months, I tried to snuff out the desire but each time the flame would flicker back to life. A quiet voice urged me to continue, yet my heart and my mind screamed, "I hate judo!"

Despite my inner conflict, I competed at the senior nationals in Michigan. I placed third behind Ed Liddie and Fred Glock. The results were encouraging: I had improved dramatically in Japan. But I still didn't have the drive and desire to continue.

Confused and desperate, I cried out to God for answers: *Lord, you know how much I struggle with judo. I no longer want any part of it! Yet at the same time, I still have this nudging in my heart to train for the 1988 Olympics. If You really want me to go, You have to give me a desire.*

Nothing changed.

I still hated judo. And I definitely couldn't imagine getting back into the grind of training six days a week for the next four years. Sure that my career had come to an end, I looked forward to life without judo.

GOD'S TURN

That night I attended our church's evening service. The speaker was Loren Cunningham, founder of Youth with a Mission, an organization that trains young people to share the gospel of Jesus Christ around the world. It was an inspiring message that normally would have inflamed my missionary zeal. Instead, I was renewed with an overwhelming passion for the Olympics. It blew my mind.

Just a few hours earlier, I didn't want anything to do with judo. Suddenly I was ready to pursue the Olympic dream. I hadn't conjured up this passion on my own; I realized this was my unique mission and assignment in life. God answered my prayer.

The next day, as I pondered what had happened, I called my old mentor, Lance Sokugawa, and asked him to lunch. I had always looked up to Lance as my judo idol. He was one of the top athletes of his time and had had a solid chance to make the 1980 Olympic team. Instead, he quit judo and helped to start a church.

As we ate, I asked him if he regretted not trying for the Olympic team. After a short pause, he responded, "Yes, I regret not continuing judo. I always wondered what would have happened if I didn't quit."

That hit me hard.

Would I regret it? Would I forever ask myself, "What would have happened if…?" At twenty-one years old, I faced a prime window of opportunity. Once it closed, I would never have another chance.

My decision to go for the Olympics became solid.

FEELING GOD'S PLEASURE

Talking with Lance reminded me of my favorite movie, *Chariots of Fire*. In 1981 it won the Academy Award for Best Picture. Eric Liddell was a Christian who ran at the 1924 Paris Olympic Games in the 400-meter event. His sister questioned his commitment to God because he was more passionate about running than preparing to go to China as a missionary. Liddell's response summed up my own feelings about competition: *"God made me for China, but God also made me fast, and when I run, I feel His pleasure."*

God made me to excel in judo. Sure, it was a unique calling, but doing judo brought Him pleasure and glory. I had to go for it!

FINDING OLYMPIC-LEVEL TRAINING

If I wanted to make the U.S. Olympic Team, I needed to train with the nation's best. San Jose State University was that team. Under the direction of Coach Yosh Uchida, they had won the collegiate national championships for a remarkable twenty-one out of twenty-four years. On the international scene, their athletes won more medals—Olympics, World Championships, World University Games, Pan American Games—than the rest of the United States combined.

Top athletes from all over the country came to San Jose State. Coach Uchida also expected everyone to graduate and succeed in his or her careers. He was in the business of making educated champions.

I arrived at San Jose State University in the fall of 1985. When I got off the plane, two students greeted me at the airport and, for my indoctrination, took me to Togo's for a pastrami sandwich. It was nice to have such a warm welcome from the students and later from the coaches as well. Immediately I felt at ease in San Jose.

Once I got settled, one of my first priorities was to find a good church. Though I often struggled in my faith, the church played a vital role in reminding me that I was competing to glorify God, not me. A dynamic pastor, Emmanuel Cannistraci, had often been a guest speaker back at my church in Hawaii. Pastor Cannistraci had a way of motivating people to commit their lives to Christ and believe for the impossible. It was exciting to sit under his leadership and grow as a Christian.

WE'RE NOT IN JAPAN ANYMORE!

On the first day of practice, I couldn't believe the country's top judo team practiced there. The location was the second floor of an old campus gym, a far cry from the spacious, temple-like *dojo* in Tokai. The place was damp, musty, and hot from the wrestlers who practiced before us. Once they left, we pulled an old canvas tarp over the wrestling mats and tucked it under to keep it secure.

I was shocked to watch the team clean the mats by taking off their *gi* tops and whirling them around, sweeping away the dust, debris and hair. It was filthy! I imagined having my face smashed into this bacteria-infested floor. The room probably hadn't had a proper cleansing since the first judo team used it forty-five years earlier.

Finally Coach Uchida came to talk to the twenty-five members of the team. "Ladies and gentlemen," he started, "you are here first and foremost to get an education. Judo will not feed you; you need to get a good education. But you are also here to become champions. For you who are new, expect to get beaten up. Hang in there, train hard every day and by the end of your four years here, you will be a tough player. Some of you may even have the opportunity to make the Olympic team."

That's what I wanted to hear. For the next few years, this one goal would consume my life. I wouldn't be satisfied until I reached the dream that had eluded me in 1984. Sure I wanted to graduate, but I was there first and foremost for judo.

GETTING BEAT BY THE COACHES

My first reality check came as soon as practice started. After training at Tokai, I felt invincible in matwork against any American opponent. I was humbled and shocked. I was choked out by an assistant coach whose prime had passed many years before.

Coach Uchida's assistants ran the practices because he was busy with a successful laboratory testing service and other business endeavors. One reason for the program's success was Coach Uchida's donations. Assistant Coach Pennington worked out with us at each practice. Off the mat he seemed like a humble and friendly guy. On the mat he was a machine. As a former middleweight in his mid-forties, he always managed to slip his hand under my chin and choke me.

My second reality check came from an even older and lighter assistant coach, Yuzo Koga. He was in his late forties so I decided to take it easy on him. Within thirty seconds, I found myself flying in the air and landing firmly on the mat from a quick *ashi barai* (foot sweep). How could this "old man" throw me so easily? That did it! No more chances! I got up to give him my best but quickly found myself on my back again from his devastating *seoi nage* (shoulder throw). In fact, for the next two years, I landed on my back every time I worked out with him.

The third slam happened when I worked out with Keith Nakasone. The one-time Olympian was now retired and out-of-shape with a bad knee. He had competed in my weight division so our workout would give me a good indication of my progress. I was in a lot more trouble than I thought. I tentatively gripped his *gi* and felt out his movements, but within fifteen seconds, he threw me effortlessly with a beautiful *uchimata* (inner thigh throw).

Not only could the coaches tell me what to do, they proved that their techniques worked. It was an excellent reminder that great judo is not just strength, stamina, and youth, but also timing and technique.

THE 1985 U.S. OPEN

My first test came in October 1985 at the U.S. Open. This tournament drew competitors from all over the world, the toughest from

Japan and Korea. It was one of two all-important tournaments for U.S. athletes because it determined rankings for the World Championship and the Olympic team trials.

In the semifinals, I faced Jung-Oh Hwang, a Korean who had won the silver medal at the 1984 Olympics in the next higher weight division. Tempers flared during the match and it almost turned into a brawl. He was the meanest competitor I had ever faced, and I was determined not to back down from his barrage of throws. I ended up losing, but I came away knowing I could compete with world-class athletes. I went on to win the next match and got a bronze medal, while the Korean lost in the finals to American Fred Glock. Little did I know but this American was going to play a key part in my future.

Freddie, as everyone called him, trained at the Olympic Training Center in Colorado Springs, Colorado. Short and scrappy, he still ranked number one. The number two man was Ed Liddie, the bronze medalist at the 1984 Olympics, a tall player who also trained at the Olympic Training Center.

With my fresh win at the U.S. Open, I had moved up in ranking to number three. I was on course to making the Olympic trials but I had two seasoned and talented players ahead of me. The Olympic trials were still more than two years away, giving me enough time to develop my skills and beat them.

THE 1986 SENIOR NATIONALS

In April 1986, after six months of intense training, I entered the U.S. Senior Nationals in Hawaii. Despite my hometown advantage, I was still beaten by Ed Liddie in the semifinals and came in third. Ed, in turn, was beaten by Fred in the finals. We remained one, two, and three in the national rankings, with me pulling up the rear.

Ed presented a formidable challenge and I just couldn't beat him. Maybe it was the first time we competed against each other in

1982: He had attempted a throw that sprained my left ankle, which left me using a cane for a week. Perhaps it was his notoriety from winning the bronze at the 1984 Olympics. Most likely, though, he was just a better and more experienced player. I had a long way to go. I needed something more in my training to get to the next level.

So that summer I returned to Tokai for two months. After being away from Japan for a year and a half, it was good to be back. This time I was comfortable with the surroundings and jumped right into training. The players still beat me but not as badly. Yes, actual progress!

INJURIES UPON INJURIES

If following Christ means bearing your cross daily, then my judo meant bearing an injury of some sort every day. Suffering was never a question of if, but of how long and how much. Many times, the athletic trainers taped one and sometimes both of my ankles. We used soft wrestling mats, where I often stubbed toes and twisted ankles. The most painful part of an ankle injury is rehabilitation: Twenty minutes of soaking in ice cold water to keep the swelling down. The first few minutes were torture until my feet went numb from the cold. That was before *and* after practice.

Most of my injuries were not major and didn't cause permanent damage. The only injury that still bothers me is my dislocated left big toe. That came from Japan.

Every spring Katsuhide Ando *sensei* from Keio University in Japan came to San Jose State to train us for the collegiate and senior nationals. He worked us over at every practice. Like all San Jose State coaches, he beat us with technique. He was also direct with his comments. In his Japanese accent, he would tell us, "I'm going to beat you up!" He then carried out that promise.

One practice while we did *newaza*, Ando *sensei* was on his back and I grabbed his pants to pull his legs to my right. My left big toe got caught in the pant opening, and I ended up tearing the ligaments and dislocating my toe. Fortunately, it popped right back into its socket but the area swelled badly and quickly turned black and blue.

Even with the immense pain I decided not to see the doctor. For weeks I hobbled about while I continued to practice. With the nationals coming up, I couldn't afford to rest and lose my edge. To this day, every time I practice I tape my toe to keep it from popping out.

My most devastating injury, however, was not one that I sustained but one that I caused. During a practice match, I competed against John Kawamoto. John and I started at San Jose State together, chose the same business major, competed in the same weight division, and worked out together every day. He was a tough and dedicated competitor who always inspired me to train harder.

During the match I attempted an *ouchi gari* (major inner reaping throw). As I swept his leg, his foot got caught in the mat, the force severely injured his right knee. In obvious pain, he hobbled off the mat and had it checked out. They diagnosed that he had torn the ligaments in his knee and required surgery. He was out of training for several months. I was devastated. Even in his leg brace and crutches, John never blamed me and always carried a cheerful disposition. John was always a team player and contributed to my success in college.

STEPPING ONTO *YOUR* MAT

It would have been much easier to quit judo and focus on graduation and a career. But knowing that I had a chance to make the Olympic team, I would have regretted not taking a risk.

Now that I am older with a family and more responsibilities, it's easy to play it safe and not take chances. I have tried this approach but life spirals downward and I lose motivation to grow and succeed.

Without risk, life becomes boring and loses purpose. All great men and women have one trait in common: They live their lives to the fullest by taking necessary risks.

What decisions do you regret, times when you "played it safe"?
What do you need to do now that will take a huge risk?

ELEVEN

One Step Shy of the Olympics

My teammates knew two Kevin Asanos: one on the mat and another off the mat. On the mat, I possessed a fighting spirit that was intense and aggressive. It was not enough just to throw my opponent onto the mat; I wanted to pound him through it. Off the mat I was totally different: quiet, reserved and timidly shy.

One of my best friends was my new roommate, Dan Hatano who had transferred from Fullerton's wrestling program to do judo at San Jose State. He too had Olympic judo aspirations and we made a great training partnership.

Four times a week we lifted weights or ran in the mornings. Five times a week we worked out with the team in the afternoon. We trained until we were ragged from the pounding we inflicted on each other. When either of us let up, the other would yell words of encouragement. Our hardcore training extended into a friendship from God.

FOOD OF CHAMPIONS

With our intense six-day-a-week training schedule, you would think we had a strict and healthy diet. I can't say that we ate balanced meals, but Dan and I ate a lot of delicious food that we made at home. Since we lived off campus, we had to shop for food and cook our own meals. Once a week we went to the same neighborhood Lucky's grocery store, went down the same aisle, and bought the same ingredients for the same meals.

Our weekly menu consisted of rib eye steak, spaghetti with spicy pork and Prego sauce, shoyu chicken, and chicken adobo with lots of garlic, vinegar, and pepper. For variety, we occasionally added pork chops with Campbell's mushroom soup, lasagna, or sweet and sour pork butt. During those two years, we never grew tired of our seven dishes. To our credit, we hardly ate any snacks, mainly because of our tight budget. By cooking together every night, we learned teamwork.

WEEKENDS IN MY SANCTUARY

On Saturdays after training, Dan usually left for the weekend and it was my chance to relax. Except for Sunday church service, I stayed in my apartment and slept. My bedroom was where I retreated to renew my physical and mental strength.

Sunday was my time to go to church and restore my spirit. The worship and message brought order to my life. It also reminded me that God was my strength, just as His Word promises: "I can do everything through Him who gives me strength" (Philippians 4:13). Those few hours gave me the boost I needed to last the week.

REALITY CHECK…AGAIN

At the 1986 U.S. Open in Colorado Springs that fall, reality came crashing in. I lost to Brazil's Sergio Pessoa in the semifinals and placed third again. There was still more than a year until the Olympic trials but I wondered if I would ever surpass Ed or Fred in points. No matter what I did, I could not get past number three.

Back in San Jose, I intensified my efforts. Every day I focused on strategy to overcome Ed and Fred and watched videos of their competitions to find their weaknesses. I had to crack what seemed impossible to become victorious!

HAWAII KID IN THE COMMUNIST BLOC

In early spring 1987, our national judo organization selected me to compete in a European tour. Our team traveled to Budapest, Hungary; then the next week to Prague, Czechoslovakia; and two weeks later, I hooked up with another team to travel to East Berlin, Germany. Traveling to three Communist bloc countries was not your typical European vacation but I felt fortunate to see what most westerners had never seen.

Being from Hawaii, I was definitely out of my element and my results in Budapest and Prague were as dreary as the snowy weather. I didn't get further than the quarterfinals. In Budapest, I faced Pessoa again and lost for the second time. With his exception, all of my competitors were Europeans. They had a different style from traditional judo, incorporating more physical wrestling moves.

EAST BERLIN

My final stop was East Germany. Of the three countries, this one left the greatest impact on my heart. To get to East Berlin, we had to fly into West Berlin, which was like any other major western European city. As we approached the graffiti-covered Berlin Wall that separated the two countries, I had an eerie feeling. The contrast was like night and day. On the west side, the road was lined with nice buildings and filled with modern cars, our own was a Mercedes-Benz taxi.

Then we passed through Checkpoint Charlie, a symbol of the Cold War with its famous demarcation line and sign that proclaimed, "YOU ARE LEAVING THE AMERICAN SECTOR." The guards who processed our visas seemed not to trust us. Every item we carried was scrutinized, as if we were smuggling something into the country. When we finally crossed over to East Berlin, a subtle gloom fell over us. The weather was the same, but on this side of the wall the sky somehow seemed darker.

In contrast to the progressive, bustling tone of West Berlin, East Berlin seemed stuck in the past. The buildings looked older and the cars were leftovers from another time. Seeing these two countries side by side gave me a clear picture of democracy and communism.

At the tournament, I made it to the semifinals and placed third. It was a tough competition and winning boosted my confidence. I was one step closer to the Olympics!

PREPPING FOR NATIONALS

Back in San Jose, the team geared up for the collegiate and senior nationals. I was the top ranked collegiate player in the nation and had never lost a match at a local tournament. My coaches selected me as captain of the team. Still, I wouldn't be satisfied until I broke into the top of the senior level.

One day at practice, as I piggybacked my partner up the stairway for conditioning, a thought flashed through my mind: *My efforts are paying off!* Every day I made small progressive improvements and with perseverance I would make it. This time the outcome would be different.

UNDONE BY MYSELF

In April 1987, I had another opportunity to prove myself against Ed and Fred at the U.S. Senior Nationals in Pittsburgh, Pennsylvania. I was emotionally and physically prepared, but I began to self-destruct mentally. It started with diarrhea in the morning from cutting weight and not eating and then bingeing after the weigh-in. Before my first match half my strength was gone. In my second match my timing was off and for my third match I barely beat a high school student. This was no ordinary student, though. It was Jimmy Pedro, Jr. who twelve years later would become the second American to win a World Championship.

By the time I faced Ed in the semifinals, I was mentally and physically drained. He dominated the match and I lost again. I watched as Ed and Fred battled for first place. Fred won again and nothing changed: Our national rankings remained with Fred in first, Ed in second, and me in third.

I was no closer to my goal than I had been two years earlier. The harder I trained and the better I became, Ed and Fred still managed to stay a step ahead. Would I miss my Olympic dream again?

BUSTING MY MENTAL BLOCK

Olympic trials were only nine months away and already I was defeated. There was no time to wallow in self-pity. The Pan American Games and World Championship trials were only a month away.

Every day I devised strategies to get the mental edge over my competition. One of the alumni at San Jose State, Rod Conduragis, stirred up the warrior within me. A two-time national champion in the early 1980s, Rod told me my fighting style was too "nice": I needed to be more physical and brutal. In other words, I needed to be meaner on the mat. This would give me the advantage I needed against my opponents.

When May 1987 rolled around, Coach Keith Nakasone and four of us from San Jose State traveled to the Olympic Training Center in Colorado Springs. My archrivals, Ed and Fred, trained there and had the double-edged advantage of a large cheering section and bodies accustomed to the high altitude.

On the first day of competition, I beat Ed by a decision in the semifinals and threw Fred for a small point in the finals. Since I ranked third, I had to compete again the next day against Fred.

Riding the momentum of my first day's success, I threw Fred with a *tomoe nage* and won the match. I had done it! I had broken through the invisible wall that had frustrated me for so long. Next up were the Pan American Games, and I couldn't wait!

"STRIPPED" OF MY WIN

After every major tournament, winners were required to take a drug test to detect any performance-enhancing drugs. Steroids had become a big problem in international competitions, and the U.S. Olympic Committee was trying to curtail its use. I had been taking medication for extreme allergies. In my carelessness, I failed to call the Olympic Committee's drug hotline to check if my prescription antihistamine was on the list. My drug test came back positive.

It was a nightmare. The Olympic Committee could ban me from all competition for one year. And if that happened, I would lose my spot on the World team and miss the opportunity to compete in the Olympic trials. I turned to Coach Keith and said, "It's no use, I'm giving up! No matter how hard I try, I keep getting knocked down." He replied, "Under no circumstances are you going to quit! We're going to fight this."

Back at San Jose, Dave Long, one of the assistant coaches invited me over to his house to help me write an appeal letter to the Olympic Committee. I was worried and discouraged. Would all of my years of hard work amount to nothing? How could this be happening to me? I thought it was my calling to compete for the Olympic team. Dave encouraged me by telling me that the team believed in me and knew that I wasn't trying to cheat the system.

It took several weeks for the Olympic Committee to make its ruling. In the meantime, I was still on the Pan American and World team and traveled to Japan for training. There was nothing left for me to do; my future hung in the balance.

On the day of the ruling, I called with my heart pounding and my palms sweating. As the doctor picked up, I held my breath. The committee had ruled in my favor and was allowing me to compete. It was a clear, inadvertent mistake and the antihistamine was not a true performance-enhancing substance. What saved me was the fact that I had listed the drug at test time, showing that I wasn't trying to hide its use. But with the good news came a stern warning: any future violation would disqualify me from competition. My heart leapt for joy! With renewed focus and confidence, I set my sights on winning.

MEETING A TRUE CHAMPION

On a stopover in Hawaii, I had a chance to meet Tommy Kono, an Olympic weightlifter who had set twenty-six world records in four weight divisions. He also had three Olympic medals in three weight divisions at the 1952, 1956 and 1960 Olympics. Tommy was one of the greatest all-time athletes in the world.

Tommy shared his experiences as an Olympian and what it took for him to become a champion. As a child, he had been frail and suffered from asthma. During World War II, he and his family had spent three years interned in Tule Lake because they were Japanese-American. During that time, he began weight training and later went on to become the best in the world.

This man was a true champion. He taught me that adversity could be a great teacher and motivator, if I would just stop pitying myself and learn from it. More than ever, I wanted to win.

PAN AM GAMES 1987

The tenth Pan American Games opened on August 8, 1987 with 4,453 athletes from thirty-eight countries. Over 80,000 spectators filled the opening ceremonies at the Indianapolis Motor Speedway. It was a thrilling taste of the upcoming Olympics.

I made it to the finals and again faced Sergio Pessoa from Brazil. He had beaten me twice, but he wouldn't beat me here! I fought my heart out and even scored, but ended up losing by a penalty for grabbing the inside of his pants. I was devastated.

At the medal ceremony, tears trickled down my face. It was the first time since I was eight years old that I cried after losing a match. As a child, I cried because my pride was hurt; this time I cried because I felt I had let down my family, teammates, and supporters. I had to redeem myself at the World Championships.

GOING TO THE MAT...WITH GOD

In the fall semester of 1987, I carried a full course load and trained for the World Championships. The stress of it all began taking a heavy toll: I developed beginning stages of ulcers and noticed that when I ran my fingers through my hair, strands would come loose. Now I had the added stress of worrying that I was balding!

My worries grew: How would I do in the upcoming competitions? After all the years of training and sacrifice, would I rise to the challenge?

Deep down inside, fear and courage grappled to gain the upper hand.

During this stressful time, I kept up the rigorous training schedule. On some days, practice went well; on other days, nothing worked. I was the captain of the team and an elite United States athlete, yet the brown belts and women were throwing me around. I was in a slump. Upset and discouraged, I hurried to the locker room, sat with my face in a towel and began to cry.

What was happening? Generally, I always felt hopeful about winning. This time I bottomed out. During my darkest despair, I sensed the Lord encouraging me. A small, still voice in my heart told me that I must continue to persevere. This was *not* the time to give up but to push beyond my limitations.

I reflected on the day when I knew the Lord gave me an over-whelming desire to train for the 1988 Olympics. If God had called me to compete, He wasn't going to leave me now when I needed Him most. My short time alone in the locker room was the encounter with God I needed to lift me up and refocus on my destiny.

WORLD CHAMPIONSHIPS 1987

In judo, the World Championships was the "Big Show." Held once every two years, it brings the best competitors from around the globe. The level of competition is on par with the Olympics. This year it was held in Essen, West Germany.

The day before my competition, Michael Swain, a San Jose State teammate won America's first World Championship. Our team was abuzz. The United States had finally broken through the top ranks. It made me think, *If Mike can do it, why can't I?*

I won my first two matches and made it to the quarterfinals where I faced Shinji Hosokawa, the 1984 Olympic gold medalist and 1985 World Champion from Japan. He was favored for the championship, and I was just another bump on the road to victory. From the onset of our match I realized why: his quick steps and hand movements made it difficult to get a solid grip. Though our match went the distance with no score, he beat me by a unanimous referee decision.

Hosokawa went on to compete in the finals, while I had a chance to compete for the bronze medal. My opponent? Sergio Pessoa.

This time would be different. Defeat is the best teacher and I had devised a new strategy based on past matches. Instead of moving forward and back, left and right, I decided to move in circles, clockwise and counterclockwise. The plan worked. I beat Pessoa soundly for the first time!

Finally, after so many years of struggle, my heart knew that I could be a champion. Not only that, others also began to speculate about the possibility of me not only making the Olympic team but receiving an Olympic medal. It was a glorious breakthrough and victory!

THE FINAL SHOT: U.S. OPEN 1987

Winning the bronze at the World Championships had no bearing on my U.S. ranking. I was still third. Fred Glock and Ed Liddie were still numbers one and two respectively. The U.S. Open was the last point tournament before the Olympic trials. It would be the ultimate destination to determine our final rankings.

At the U.S. Open I dominated the preliminary rounds and made it to finals. Ed had beaten Fred, so the championship was between Ed and me. The winner would be the number one ranked athlete in the country.

One minute into the match, I caught Ed near the sideline for a *waza-ari* (half-point) with my favorite throw, *tomoe nage*. We stared at each other in shared surprise. I had never been able to throw him with such a high score. When the match ended I had finally beaten Ed Liddie. **I ranked number one!**

Of course, my victory was short-lived: A rematch was set for the Olympic trials.

UP FOR THE OLYMPIC TRIALS

The first Olympic trials came quickly on a cold Saturday morning in February 1988 at the Olympic Training Center in Colorado Springs, Colorado. A win here would secure my spot on the Olympic team. I made it to the finals. Fred and Ed squared off, and Ed won. He and I would face off in the finals. It was the showdown I had dreamed about. Each time I imagined the match, I always came out the winner.

For the first three minutes there was no score, until Ed caught me for a *koka* (smallest point) and from there I had to chase him. I couldn't get the advantage and the match ended with Ed as the victor. Walking back to bow out, my head spun. Surely, I was having a nightmare! I couldn't believe I had lost the match. I walked in a daze, not knowing what to do or think; devastated. So close to clinching my dream of making the Olympic team, and yet in a moment I had let it slip away. All the years of training and sacrifice flashed before my eyes.

How could this have happened?

FINAL TRIALS...LAST CHANCE

Three months down the road, I would face off with Ed again at the final Olympic trials. I was very much in the hunt for the Olympics, but mentally and emotionally, I was defeated. The pressure was overwhelming. I had dedicated eighteen years of my life to judo, with the last five years solely focused on making the Olympic team. I worked out six days a week, many times twice a day, all year long. My body had paid for the relentless training with constant injuries and a severely irritating, chronic rash.

Our middle-class family had sacrificed tens of thousands of dollars for travel, training and education. I had put college and career on hold. So much of my life had been invested into making the Olympic team that to come so close, only to have it ripped out of my grasp, was hard to handle.

Training for three more months seemed an impossible burden to my weary soul.

STEPPING ONTO *YOUR* MAT

Throughout my life my greatest successes have come when I have been part of a team. Without my supporters, coaches, and team-mates, I know I wouldn't have excelled in judo. They pushed and encouraged me when I wanted to take it easy or give up. I needed the support, accountability, and strength a team provides.

Today, I team up with others often – in everything from business to child rearing and even in coaching judo. In the long run, a team is more effective and powerful than an individual working alone. Besides, it's more enjoyable to share your life with others as you strive for a common goal.

Who do you have around you that can help you to be more successful?
Better yet, to whom are you extending yourself to make them successful?

TWELVE

Just Twelve Inches

When I returned to San Jose, I moped around the apartment and spent most of my time in bed reading novels. I hid in a fantasy world to escape my latest defeat. Then Dan came to my side. For two years, we had roomed, trained, eaten, and played together. In my deepest doldrums, he lifted me up.

"We are going to win!" Dan proclaimed at 6:50 A.M. on a Monday morning as he dragged me out of bed. Unfortunately, Dan no longer had a chance of making the Olympic team, so when he said "we," he meant that he would see *me* to the Olympics. This was the start of my three-month training for the Olympic trials. Thanks to his kick in my rear, I snapped out of my stupor and got back on track. Literally.

MENTALLY TRAINING TO WIN

For the next ninety days, Dan and my teammates pushed me to my limits. Mornings were reserved for running, bicycling, jumping rope, and lifting weights. In the afternoons, we concentrated on technique and conditioning. Evenings were dedicated to strategizing and watching video clips of my opponents.

If I wanted to make the Olympic team, I also needed to train mentally. I studied books on mental preparation and toughness.

Until then, no one had taught me to train my mind to win. So I made up an exercise to test my attitude about myself.

I went to the mirror and looked into my eyes. As silly as I felt, I wanted to see if a champion was looking back at me. Looking intently, I said, "You are a champion. You are a great judo player." I burst out laughing. "Who are you kidding? Look at you. You're not a champion!" I had a long way to go before I could believe in me.

PEAKING PHYSICALLY & MENTALLY

The three months between trials went by quickly. Each team member was training for his own goal of winning at nationals, but they also focused on my goal of making the Olympic team. Every day they gave me a word of encouragement and pushed me to my limit. Every practice they took dozens of falls to help me sharpen my throws. One guy took so many falls that it rubbed his neck raw!

As the trials grew closer, I knew I was peaking both physically and mentally. I was in the best shape of my life and was completely focused. I could finally look at myself and say with conviction, "Kevin, you are a champion! You are a great judo player! You are the best!" Something inside finally clicked. I was ready.

THE SECOND & FINAL OLYMPIC TRIALS

The day of the trials, May 14, 1988, finally arrived. That morning, as I warmed up, Coach Keith gave me one final encouragement: "Kevin, this is what you've been training for all these years. You're ready. Go out there and beat this guy to the punch. When he goes down to the mat, take him. Go get 'em!" With that he slapped my lower back three times then sent me onto the mat.

All the years of training came down to this competition. All the years of sacrifice and hard work would either pay off with a spot on the Olympic team or end in disappointment. I had no choice but to win.

Ed and I were first to compete in our best of three matches. When the announcer called our names, I walked onto the mat with complete confidence, even flashing a smile at the officials watching from the head table. My smile said, "Watch me win."

Our match started and Ed and I quickly engaged aggressively. For most of the match, neither side gained a clear advantage. By the end of the five minutes, there was still no score. It came to a decision by the referees and judges and they awarded the win to Ed. I stepped off the mat in disbelief. Was this going to be a repeat of defeat?

As we waited for the second round, I glanced at Ed who sat looking relaxed and confident. Though I should've been concerned, something was happening inside of me. I knew I was going to win the tournament.

ROUND TWO

For the next match, I changed my game plan and looked more serious. I didn't flash my smile. The referee shouted, *"Hajime!"* and we attacked. Again, neither of us scored for a very long five minutes, but this time I was clearly more aggressive and won by decision. We were even at one each with one more match to go.

Again I glanced at Ed during the break. This time he was standing up, looking more focused and intense. I sat on the bleachers knowing that it was my day. It had come down to this final match to determine who was going to the Olympics and who was going home. It was the biggest match of my career.

We stepped onto the mat with sheer determination on our faces and waited for the referee's *"Hajime!"* We flew at each other full force. For the first one-and-a-half minutes, we went back and forth with no clear advantage. As we moved close to going out of bounds, Ed grabbed me behind the back and entered into a *sumi-gaeshi* (corner reversal throw). The referee scored it a *yuko* (second smallest point). Immediately, the referee called *matte* (stop) because we went out of bounds.

In the few seconds it took to get up and go back to the center, I thought, *It's over! There's no way that I can get Ed back. It was a good experience, but it wasn't meant to be. I'll go back to San Jose and move on with life.* At the same instant, my mind fought to refocus: **I could still win, if I didn't give up!**

I was puzzled, however, when the referee and judges stopped for a short conference. After the judges sat down again, the referee cancelled the score. He turned to Ed and pointed to the out of bounds, giving him a *chui* (second smallest penalty point). Apparently, when Ed had entered the throw, more than half of his body was out of bounds, and that was a penalty. I saw the disbelief in his eyes. It was the same disbelief mirrored in my own.

Suddenly and unbelievably, I was in control of the match.

For the next three-and-a-half minutes I worked to maintain my lead. When the buzzer finally rang, I had won the match, only by that penalty. I couldn't believe it: **I had made the Olympic team!**

After the upset, Ed congratulated me, saying, "Go get 'em, Kev!" He wished me the best at the Olympics. Despite our intense rivalry over the years, he displayed true sportsmanship and character.

THE FINAL DIFFERENCE

That afternoon I went back to the dorms and took a shower, still overwhelmed. As the warm water beat down on my shoulders, my mind drifted through the phases of my judo career. Many times I had been weak and vulnerable, and had doubted God's plan for my life. I asked God to forgive me and thanked Him for using me to bring Him glory. Filled with humility and gratitude, I broke down and cried.

It's amazing how God can humble me, even after winning a spot on the Olympic team. A few days after beating Ed, I viewed the video of our match. Had Ed been inside the boundary by just *twelve inches*, he would have won.

My victory was not about my glory and gratification. Neither was it about my superior talent. When it was all said and done, it was a matter of God gaining all glory.

STEPPING ONTO *YOUR* MAT

We have all had "twelve-inches of grace" in our lives: times when things could have gone either way. I won at the Olympic trials by a mere 12-inch penalty. I can't take credit for the win. No doubt I dedicated many years to judo, but ultimately God gave me the gift. He also brought people who helped me to reach my goal.

Today whenever and wherever I succeed, I realize God is in control. It's not about me, but about a great God working through me.

What moments have you experienced that relate with my explanation of "twelve-inches of grace"? Could you see God working in the situation?

THIRTEEN

Enjoy the Journey

After making the Olympic team I returned home to Hawaii for a short rest. Without knowing it, I had become the first judo player born and raised in Hawaii to make an Olympic team. I also had the opportunity of becoming the first gold medalist in judo from the U.S. I needed time to unwind from the stress and pressure.

It wasn't until my trip to Tbilisi, Georgia, in the then Soviet Union that I began to focus on the Olympic Games.

TERRIBLE TBILISI

Among athletes, Tbilisi had a bad reputation for a terrible triple threat: bad food, poor accommodations and brutal competition. It was considered one of the toughest events in the European tour; elite players from around the world joined the top Soviet athletes to compete for their chance to make their respective Olympic teams.

When I arrived, I realized that despite the Cold War, I had a wonderful opportunity to learn about the region. All of the negative things I had heard were not true, other than the tough competition, of course. I got to visit a scenic point in the mountains overlooking the city. I paused to enjoy the greenery and was reminded that God is the creator of beauty and splendor. It is we humans who, in our own selfish ambition, bring division and strife. With this experience, my attitude toward "the enemy" changed into compassion for the people.

Back at our hotel, the Soviet athletes were eager to meet us and came to our room to sell and barter their Russian wares. They offered caviar, beautiful woodcraft boxes, dolls, vodka, and athletic apparel in exchange for American-made goods and U.S. dollars. They were friendly, wonderful people full of lively camaraderie.

BACK TO BUSINESS

Once competition started, however, it was all business. Each round, I faced a Soviet, each physically strong and almost machine-like. It was unnerving to see them come at me, one after another, with full force but no emotion. Surprisingly, I beat each one and advanced to the finals. No American had ever won a medal at this tournament and here I was fighting for the gold.

I faced an up-and-coming young Russian, Fedor Lazarenko, who had come out of nowhere to beat the top Russians. In the end he proved to be more aggressive and won the match by a close decision. I had come in second.

The loss revealed a self-esteem problem. In the tournament, my competitors saw me as a formidable opponent. Lazarenko's coach told him he had no chance of winning and to simply do his best. On the contrary, I saw myself as an inexperienced underdog, lucky to have won the bronze at the World Championships. That negative self-image kept me from performing at top potential.

LOVE STRUCK

One of the most significant events of my life happened in Tbilisi. While relaxing, I thought about my upcoming training in Japan. Thoughts of a girl named Mari Kawamura came to mind. We had met in 1983 at Shinjuku Shalom Church. I had observed her from a distance, and except for occasional conversations, we had never connected.

Mari was an exceptionally talented and beautiful young woman. She was born in Japan but, because of her father's business in audio manufacturing, she had spent six years in Chicago and four years in West Germany. She became equally fluent in English and German as well as her own native tongue. She graduated top of her class from a prestigious Japanese university and was quickly hired by the Bank of Tokyo.

Oddly, while I was focused on training, thoughts of Mari kept breaking my concentration. *What is she doing? Is she still attending the same church?* If there was ever a dream girl to marry, it would be her. Sure, she was out of my reach. My chance of winning the gold at the Olympics was better than winning her heart. *Oh well,* I thought, *What do I have to lose?* I planned to visit Shinjuku Shalom and ask her out. If she wasn't there or turned me down, at least I would know the answer. Then I could fully concentrate on the Olympics.

GET ME TO THE CHURCH!

Right after Tbilisi, we headed for Japan to train with the top teams. On the very first Sunday, I went straight to Shinjuku Shalom Church. I walked in and sat close to the front. After the singing, the pastor asked us to turn around and greet one another. When I turned to say hello to the person behind me, it was Mari!

I greeted her and mentioned that I wanted to talk with her afterwards. For the rest of the service I couldn't concentrate on anything except mustering up the courage to ask her out. Sure I had competed against the top athletes in the world, but I was much more nervous about facing this phenomenal woman.

When the service finished, I took a deep breath, turned around, and got to the point: "Mari, I'm only going to be in town for a short time while I'm training, but would you like to go out to dinner with me?" I half-hoped she would say no so I wouldn't have to think about her and could concentrate on the Olympics.

Without hesitation she said, "Yes, I'd like that." I couldn't believe my ears. I had a date with the most beautiful and charming girl in the world!

For the next few days I couldn't concentrate. In the mornings, we trained with the Tokyo police team; in the afternoons, we rotated between Nihon University, Nippon Taiku University and Kokushi-kan University. They were the best in the country, but I couldn't get my mind off of Mari. All I could think about was our date on Thursday night.

The day finally arrived. We went out to a *yakitori* restaurant. I had hoped to take her to the top of one of the tallest buildings in Tokyo, but it was closed. We settled for a nearby hole-in-the-wall on the second floor of an old building. The smoke from the grills and a lot of cigarettes combined to permeate the room. This was not the picture of romance I had envisioned for our first date.

While most of the patrons filled up with beer and whiskey, we enjoyed our water and several small dishes. It wasn't fine dining but nothing mattered as long as I was with Mari, the most mesmerizing woman in the world.

GETTING THROWN FOR LOVE

On the exterior Mari seemed shy and reserved, but on the inside was a woman full of ambition. "Mari," I asked, "what are your dreams?"

With conviction, she replied, "Part of me wants to prove to the male-dominated society in Japan that I am just as capable and competent as any man to be successful in business." Then she softened up. "On the other hand, I also studied Portuguese in college; I'd like to go to Brazil and do missions in the Amazon jungle." Here I thought I was being bold to be a missionary in Japan, but she had me beat by her willingness to go anywhere for Jesus.

The magical night ended too soon and I had to say goodnight. I walked her to the station and waved goodbye as her train departed. That evening, I fell in love.

EVERYTHING FALLING INTO PLACE

After two weeks, the rest of the team returned to the United States, but I stayed for another two weeks to train at Tokai University. Five years earlier when I had first arrived at Tokai, I had been a practice dummy. This time was different. Sato *sensei* had fulfilled his promise to transform me into a U.S. national champion. As I worked out with the Tokai team, I could see my hard work had paid off.

Although I was finally successful, spiritually I struggled. I made mistakes that I was deeply ashamed of and often lived a selfish life. *How could I say I was a committed Christian, yet live in a way I knew was not pleasing to Him?*

This inner struggle made my journey even tougher. By God's grace and mercy, He patiently waited for me to submit so He could work true success in my life. After making the Olympic team, I finally came to my senses, surrendered my stubbornness, and returned to God. My new clear conscience was one more facet that fell into place in preparation for the Olympics.

WINNING WITHIN

Part of the joy of success – something I had not realized until this point – was the journey. Once I had made the Olympic team, I decided to train hard but to also enjoy the process. This opportunity would only come once in my lifetime, and I didn't want to waste it and later regret not enjoying my experience.

A few days before I left Japan, I walked Mari back to her apartment and asked her what she thought about competition. She had been an avid tennis player throughout high school and college.

"When I compete," she said, "I don't focus on my opponent. I focus on myself to see how hard I can push myself to reach for the ball. When my body feels like giving up, I dig deep and strive constantly to be the best player I can be."

Her answer amazed me. It was what my dad had preached to me for so many years: **to love my opponents and compete against myself.** I had never fully grasped what he meant until Mari explained her mindset. I finally understood!

My true opponent was not the guy I faced but the competitor I became when I stepped on the mat.

The statement stirred up many questions: *Could I train my spirit, mind, and body to be in top form? Could I go the distance in the face of any opposition, pain, or fatigue? Did I have the courage to overcome self-imposed fears and doubts? Did I have the character to win humbly and lose graciously?* I realized that I would be a true champion if I could answer these questions faithfully as I strived for Olympic gold. Win or lose, as long as I left everything on the mat, I could be proud.

LAST STOP HAWAII

I was less than two months away from the biggest event in my life, yet all I could think about was a captivating woman, Mari. I was in love. If I were assured that I could marry her, I would gladly have given up my spot on the Olympic team. Wisely, she was hesitant to give me her heart. Unimpressed by my athletic accomplishments, Mari was more interested in one thing: Did I really love her or was it an emotional fling?

Though I savored every moment with Mari, I was glad to go home. I needed to stay focused and couldn't while we were in the same country. On my way back to San Jose, I stopped in Hawaii for a final break. The Hawaii judo community buzzed as the first Hawaii boy headed for the Olympics and my week was spent giving newspaper, radio, and television interviews. Hawaii was rallying behind one of her sons and I was elated to have the extra moral support.

During my stopover, I also visited our church's college camp. The speaker called me up for prayer, saying, "Kevin, you need to win the gold." He confirmed that God did not promise I would win, but my judo would bring Him glory on an international platform.

After the camp, I carried three specific goals with me to Seoul. First, to give God all of the glory from my competition, regardless of the outcome. Second, to give my very best. Third, to treat the Olympic Games like a big celebration for my eighteen years of hard work. I was ready!

SEND OFF TO OLYMPIC VILLAGE

The San Jose State Judo Team gathered at the San Francisco airport to send off Mike Swain and me. Though only two of us were going to Seoul, the whole team worked hard to help us make it to the Olympics. Judo is an individual sport, but my teammates enabled me to excel to heights I never could have achieved alone. When one succeeded, we all succeeded.

Before boarding, my roommate Dan and I embraced as he wished me luck. For the past two years, he had been there for me in every step of training and life. Though he wasn't going to Seoul, in my heart I knew we were challenging the world together.

STEPPING ONTO *YOUR* MAT

If I could change one thing about my judo career, it would be to enjoy the journey more. At times I was so focused, intense, and consumed with winning. However, the true value of my Olympic experience was not in the destination but in the journey.

Today, in the hectic and sometimes stressful days of raising a family, growing my business, and contributing to society, I remind myself to enjoy the journey.

Life is too short to be too serious.

What area(s) in your life are you taking too seriously?
In what ways can you start to enjoy your family, friends, and life?

FOURTEEN

Go for the Gold

How awesome to be a part of the Olympic Games! After all these years of dreaming about making the Olympic team, it was now a reality. As we flew into Seoul, spirits were high. Then, upon our arrival, it seemed as if all of Korea had graciously come out to greet us.

Olympic posters, banners, and flags adorned the city in an enormous, nationwide celebration. Millions of dollars had been spent to upgrade the city of Seoul. Even threat of invasion by the North Koreans, as evidenced by the armed guards posted around the airport and at athletic venues, couldn't stifle the celebratory spirit of the Olympics.

OLYMPIC OPENING CEREMONIES

The opening of the 1988 Olympics was a huge party for the world to enjoy. More than 10,000 athletes from 161 countries waited outside the stadium to march in, and everyone became restless knowing we were missing the festivities inside. When the time came for the U.S.A athletes to enter, we became like kids released from school for summer.

We stormed into a stadium filled with 100,000 cheering spectators. As we paraded around the track, I was excited, overjoyed, awed, and at the same time humbled. I was privileged to represent my country and to be counted among the top athletes in the world. It is one thing to watch the opening ceremonies on television and another to march on the field. Nothing can match the feeling of being there.

After the ceremonies, we were reprimanded by the U.S. delegation for our overly-spirited display. No doubt I was in the guilty party. In my exuberance, a security guard had to escort me back onto the track after I tried to snap shots of the team's celebration.

Except for one small mishap, the opening ceremonies had been a success. It happened when they had released hundreds of doves to symbolize peace. The organizers did not realize the doves would hang around to watch the rest of the show. Some decided to sit on the rim of the giant Olympic torch that was about to be lit. Those unfortunate doves became a burnt offering for the opening festivities.

AN INTERNATIONAL FEAST

Once the Olympics started, we started light workouts to stay sharp. When I jumped on the scale I found that I was eight pounds overweight. For the next seven days I worked out wearing sweats under my judo *gi* to lose water weight while starving my body of food and liquids. At the international dining hall, I couldn't enjoy the wonderful ethnic foods—German wiener schnitzel, Chinese steamed vegetables, Italian pasta, Argentinean meat, French desserts, and my favorite Korean delicacies including kalbi, bibimbap, and traditional kim chee. This spicy menu was offered for breakfast, lunch and dinner. While others ate to their hearts' content, I had limited servings of fruits and vegetables.

Other than the hunger pangs and my dry thirst, everything else was enjoyable. Our free time was devoted to a side "competition" at Itaewon, a shopper's paradise. Store clerks offered us the best shopping bargains. Sometimes I won and walked away with a good deal, like the leather jacket I bought for my roommate. Other times I lost and was taken, like the custom-made leather shoes that fell apart a month later while I was walking in the rain.

WEIGH IN

That I was at the Olympic Games began to sink in. This was not a dream. Almost a decade earlier, I couldn't understand why my dad made me return to judo. It is amazing to see that when we submit ourselves to God's purpose, He orchestrates events and outcomes we could never dream for ourselves. I met many other Christians at the Olympic Village Chapel who encouraged me to compete at my best.

One of the chaplains took me aside and said, "Kevin, if you don't compete to win the gold, there is no sense in competing at all. You need to go out there to win." Those few words helped to bring my eighteen years of preparation to one focal point. I was ready for my competition that Sunday evening.

The evening before my competition day I jumped on the scale and weighed just below 132 pounds. The official weigh-in was set for the next morning, but I had reached my goal and celebrated with a few sips of water before bed. As I lay there trying to sleep, my mouth was parched and dry, and hunger pains gnawed at my stomach. Even so, I was energized. Tomorrow was going to be the biggest competition of my life.

By Sunday morning, September 25, I was lean, mean, and hungry. The weigh-in room was blanketed in silence as thirty-seven players, clad only in underwear and nametags around their necks, sized one another up for competition. The world's top athletes were all present, seven of whom I had lost to previously. Each loss had spurred me to improve. Instead of being intimidated, I anticipated victory.

I stepped on the scale and weighed in just below 132 pounds. After clearing my first hurdle, I headed for the cafeteria. After a few hours of rest and relaxation, I would be ready to rumble. I was in the best shape of my life—physically, mentally, emotionally, and spiritually. If there was ever a day to do well, this was my day.

GAME TIME

The afternoon came quickly and we made our way to Changchung Gymnasium. It was an evening competition, my first ever, and undoubtedly corresponded to local TV prime time. Of all the sports, Korea had the best chance to win the gold in judo. There were a lot of high hopes for Koreans to sweep this event before the world.

The air in the arena was festive and charged, as all 7,000 seats were filled. Lights illuminated the raised platform where every throw, pin, choke, and arm-lock would be captured on film. In a few minutes, I would be competing before a worldwide audience. Cheerleaders, musicians, and drummers lined the circular arena, ready to cheer on their fellow countryman Kim Jae-Yup. Armed guards were also posted to protect the athletes and prevent any rioting or civil unrest. I joked that they were there to ensure the Koreans made it to the finals. It seemed more like a pro-wrestling match than a traditional judo competition. To top it all off, it was Korean Thanksgiving Day, and the nation seemed determined that no one was going to spoil their celebration.

As I loosened up on deck, I felt all the jitters and nervousness disappear. Amazingly, I was filled with a calm and peace I had never experienced during competition. At that moment, I believe God spoke to me in a small voice, saying, "Kevin, you're going to do well today." What "well" meant, I had no idea, but I knew it would be special. Tears sprung to my eyes as I encountered the presence of God. All I could say was, "Wow!" I quickly gathered my composure as I was set to begin my competition in a few short minutes.

NO WARM WELCOME

When I stepped onto the mat, the audience greeted me with a resounding chorus of boos. It surprised and confused me. I didn't think there was any reason for my unpopularity in Korea.

I later realized that the Koreans had booed me and Japan's Shinji Hosokawa because of our Japanese heritage. The Koreans had a fierce rivalry with their Japanese neighbors, dating back to Japan's colonial rule over Korea from 1910 to 1945. And, since judo is traditionally a Japanese sport, the Koreans wanted to prove that they could beat the Japanese at their own game.

FIRST MATCH: PETER SEDIVAK

I put the negative vibe aside and focused on my first opponent, Peter Sedivak. The Czechoslovakian had beaten me two out of three times, including the 1986 World University Championships where he almost choked me unconscious. Luckily, I had rolled out of bounds before I blacked out. He won by decision.

In the first minutes of our rematch, my contact lens folded in my eye, and I had to ask the referee to stop the match. The crowd had a good laugh as I fumbled to stick the lens back into my eye. I had never been able to master this feat without a mirror, and here I was in front of a world audience and thousands in live attendance, doing the impossible.

Once we continued the match, Sedivak lifted me completely off the mat with his *hanegoshi* (spring hip throw). It would have been a perfect throw had it not been for split-second acrobatic maneuvering. I caught Sedivak for a *koka* (smallest point) with a *kouchi gari* (minor inner reaping throw) and remained dominant for the rest of the match to win.

In spontaneous celebration I raised my hands, flashed a smile and waved to the audience as I walked off the mat. This was highly uncharacteristic; I am usually reserved after winning. This competition was different for me and felt like a big party, designed for fun and joy. The audience was indifferent, except for a small American delegation led by USA Judo President Frank Fullerton. My mom's cheers seemed to make up for the silent majority: I could see her screaming my name as I walked off the mat. She waved a huge American flag with her right hand and held a giant hand-shaped sponge on her left that said "Kev #1." She was my greatest fan.

Coach Uchida and at least ten other San Jose State alumni were in the crowd. Alumnus Steve Bonior paid particular attention to my disposition before and after my matches. The thing that impacted him most was realizing that a Godly person could be a tough competitor and winner. He had always felt that Christians were weak-willed and therefore incapable of becoming champions. Steve told me he was on a spiritual journey to find God and my performance helped bring him one step closer to Jesus Christ.

SECOND & THIRD ROUNDS

In the second round, I faced Kan Lee from Hong Kong. From the start, Lee came with full force. He shot an *uchimata* (inner thigh throw) that I quickly side-stepped and countered with a *tai otoshi* (body drop throw) for *ippon* (full point).

Then I faced Tsay-Chwan Sheu from Taipei, Taiwan. In the first thirty seconds, I attempted my *tomoe nage* (circle throw) and the referee gave him a score. I was confused with the call, but I had to catch up. The judges soon overruled the score, and I quickly scored a *yuko* (second smallest point) then side-stepped his *seoi nage* (shoulder throw) and threw him with an *uchimata* for *ippon*.

Though I easily won the first three matches, it was clear that the Koreans were cheering for my opponents by booing me each time. Nevertheless, I advanced to the semifinal match with Japan's Hosokawa. Hosokawa was the man I needed to beat in order to compete for the gold medal. Statistically I had little chance of winning: he was the captain of the Japanese judo team, the 1984 Olympic gold medalist, and the 1985 World Champion. In the 1987 World Championships, I had lost to Hosokawa in the quarterfinals by decision. In my heart I knew this time I would emerge the victor.

Neither of us anticipated the crowd's reaction to a match-up between a Japanese and Japanese-American. We had both been booed in every preliminary bout, but suddenly, the Koreans chanted "U.S.A., U.S.A., U.S.A.!" The arena reverberated with enthusiasm for the new favorite: me! To have an entire country cheering for me was unbelievable. I had never experienced this level of support, even when I had competed in America at the Pan American Games. Left with a choice, I was less Japanese than Hosokawa, so I became the favorite. I couldn't lose!

SEMIFINALS: ASANO V. HOSOKAWA

The announcer called our names after a short rest. Our faces portrayed contrasting mindsets—his showed fierce determination and mine displayed quiet assurance. Competitive judo is much like an ancient Japanese samurai battle. One man emerged the winner and the other would be killed. The weight of Japan rested on Hosokawa's shoulders.

As we turned to face each other before stepping onto the mat, I noticed Hosokawa's intensity. I spontaneously flashed a grin, saying to myself, "Buddy, you're going down today!" But my mind sprang into action as the referee yelled, "*Hajime!*"

We went into all-out assault. I lifted Hosokawa off the mat several times with my *tomoe nage* only to have each one blocked. Hosokawa then cornered me and, before I could get a solid grip, he attempted *tomoe nage*. The throw was so fast and smooth that I couldn't block it. Instead, in a split-second reaction, I did a cartwheel, spun on my head, and landed on my feet, successfully thwarting his throw. It amazed everyone including myself. My only thought was, *Get going, Kevin! You're behind!*

Throughout the five-minute match, neither of us was able to score. At the buzzer, I stuck out my hand and gave Hosokawa a congratulatory high-five. It was in the hands of the referee and judges, and I knew it was close and could go either way. In celebration, I raised my hand in victory and waved to my newfound Korean friends. My anticipation of victory puzzled even the Japanese television announcer.

We stepped back to the starting position to await the outcome. When the referee asked for judges' decision, one raised the red flag for Hosokawa and the other lifted the white flag for me. That left the decision to the referee. He immediately awarded the win to me. All pandemonium broke loose as my adopted country went wild in celebration. I lifted my arms again. I had made it to the finals!

THE FINAL MATCH FOR OLYMPIC GOLD

There was a lengthy break before the final competition. Win or lose, I was going to get a medal, but I had to concentrate on the gold. While I rested and kept focus, Korean Kim Jae-Yup and his coaches scrambled to study videotapes of my matches. They hadn't prepared for me to beat Hosokawa. In fact, the judo world was stunned that I had won. This was the biggest upset at the tournament, although I wasn't surprised. In preparation for the Olympics, I had pictured myself again and again winning the gold.

I had faced Kim before at the 1986 World University Championships and lost. This Korean had an impressive record: a silver medal at the 1984 Olympics and gold at the 1987 World Championships. Amazingly, I wasn't nervous or tense. The same voice that spoke to me at the beginning of the competition had carried me to the finals. I was only one win away from becoming the Olympic champion.

When I returned to the arena, the crowd was charged with excitement. The cheerleaders and drummers led the Korean spectators in a deafening war chant. The rhythmic sound of "U.S.A., U.S.A.,

U.S.A.!" had quickly been replaced with "Kim Jae-Yup, Kim Jae-Yup, Kim Jae-Yup!" In my ears, it rang more like "Kill That Bum! Kill That Bum!" My only consolation was that the audience was so occupied with their own hero that they didn't bother to taunt me.

"HAJIME!"

Fifty feet across the mat I watched Kim prepare by slapping his own face and pulling at his hair. I hit my legs and stepped onto the mat, ready for battle. We bowed, stepped forward, and waited for the referee's yell. At "*Hajime!*" we unleashed.

I started combat by attempting my favorite, *tomoe nage*. I almost scored when Kim fell to his knees. From there, we immediately began to grapple on the mat. The crowd's cheers ebbed and erupted with the action, but I remained undaunted. For three minutes we went blow-for-blow attempting throws, pins, chokes, and arm-locks. We were even until we went to the ground.

Kim lay on his back with my back to his chest and lower body between his legs, when he started to choke me. To counter, I grabbed his fingers near my neck and squeezed to prevent him from moving his hand under my chin. After several attempts, the referee pointed to my hand and gave me a *shido* (smallest penalty point). I was surprised, thinking that my action was a legitimate defense. The referee didn't see it that way, and I found myself behind by a penalty.

At that point Kim turned up the pressure and continued offensively to keep me from catching him. As the last seconds ticked away, Kim raised his hands in victory and the crowd went wild. At the final buzzer, the decibel level in the arena became deafening as Korea celebrated their Olympic gold medalist. Overcome with emotion, Kim dropped to the mat and buried his face in his hands.

MATCH OVER: VICTORY!

I stood there in wonder and amazement. I had just completed the match of my life. Over the years, I had always visualized raising my arms after winning at the Olympics. So as I walked back to the line, instinctively I lifted my hands as champion. A photographer captured the scene with my arms triumphantly in the air and Kim, on the ground, crying into his hands. The picture was published in newspapers throughout the United States, including one which underscored it with the caption, "Can you find the gold medalist? If you said Kevin Asano, you would be incorrect."

To the world, Kevin Asano was the silver medalist. In my heart I had captured the gold. There was no disappointment for me because I had delivered my very best. And as I walked off the mat, I held my head high.

While the Koreans chaotically celebrated their champion, I quietly expressed gratitude to the Lord for allowing me victory at the Olympics.

THE MEDAL CEREMONY

When we proceeded onto the mat to receive our medals, the arena was filled to capacity. All of Korea wanted to witness Kim receive their second Olympic gold medal. He surprised everyone when he appeared dressed in a traditional Korean costume. The crowd went crazy for their new world champion.

I stood on the winners' platform to receive my Olympic silver medal, glancing up to thank God for bringing me to this place of glory. Who would have thought that this Japanese-American boy from Hawaii – deemed too small, too weak, too young, and too inexperienced – would one day stand on the pinnacle of Olympic success?

At that moment all of the hardships and setbacks of my career faded as I watched the American flag held high. I was a champion.

No one could take that away from me. The dream my father planted in my heart twelve years earlier had transformed into a calling from God and came to pass in an exciting and remarkable way—a way even I could never have dreamed or imagined.

STEPPING ONTO *YOUR* MAT

How big are your dreams?

The problem many of us have is not that we do not dream, but that our dreams are not big enough. Even now fear and disbelief try to immobilize me. I constantly have to remind myself that God wants to use me in a greater way than what I'm thinking and living.

God gives all of us talents, abilities, and a unique calling. However, only you can choose what you will do with your life. You can take the journey of least resistance by allowing fear and doubt to keep you in your place. Or you can hear from God, step out in faith, and go for the gold.

What is your dream? Is it big enough?

David Finch

Final match at the Olympics after losing to Kim... but in my heart I won the gold medal because I gave it my best.

My early days of judo in Okinawa.

The late Fukushima sensei and myself in Hawaii.

*Training at Tokai University with
National Champion Sekimizu.*

*Training partner and roommate Dan Hatano
at San Jose University.*

Enroute to the finals against Sedivak of Czechoslovakia.

*My favorite throw, tomoe nage, on
Hosokawa of Japan.*

David Finch

Fight to the end against World and reigning Olympic Champion Hosokawa.

David Finch

Giving all the glory to God.

Seoi nage drive against 1987 World Champion Kim of Korea.

Down to the wire with Kim in the Olympic finals.

David Finch

My journey ends at the 1988 Olympic Medal Ceremony.

Steven Nohara

Myself with Fukushima Sensei and his former student
Olympian, Keith Nakasone.

Steven Nohara

My beautiful family: Rena, Mari, Maya, and Anna
(left to right).

FIFTEEN

The Journey Continues

The next morning I went to the Olympic Chapel to pray. I thanked God for the opportunity to compete, knowing it was His design and call that brought me to win a silver medal. I wanted to make sure that my life counted for God.

"God, I want to give You the glory. Help me to use this medal to share about Your wonderful purpose and plan for everyone who is willing to open their hearts to You. Use my life, Lord, in any way that pleases You."

After forty-five minutes, I decided to head back for breakfast. I came to a bridge that overlooked the Olympic Village and stopped to take in the wonder of it all. My mind drifted over the years of my judo career, one that started when I stepped onto the mat as a seven-year-old boy in Okinawa and ended when I stepped off the mat eighteen years later in Seoul, Korea.

While standing there, I experienced an amazing wonder: With my eyes closed, I saw a picture of an open book. A moment later, a hand reached down and turned the page of this book. As the page turned, I noticed that it was the end of one chapter and the beginning of a new one. Right away I understood it was the book of my life. God was calling me to end my judo career because He had a new chapter prepared for me. I wept as deep emotions flooded my soul. The image slowly faded away.

As I walked off the bridge, I was excited for the plans God had for my future.

STEPPING ONTO *YOUR* MAT

It has been many years since I stood on that bridge overlooking the Olympic Village. Since then I have walked through other deep valleys and high mountaintops. Yet more than ever, I am confident that God has great plans for my future.

Regardless of your current situation, past mistakes and failures, or personal shortcomings, God has a wonderful plan for your life. He has plans to prosper you and to give you hope and a future. With this future you have the wonderful opportunity to make a positive impact in the world.

Are you willing to allow God to give you a future and a hope?
If so, please read on…

SIXTEEN

True Success

An Olympic victory was not just my dream; it was my destiny and God's plan for His glory.

I devoted eighteen years of my life in judo to reach the epitome of sports success. My energy and focus went into an ultimate goal of winning the gold medal at the Olympic Games. To this day, much of my thinking and paradigms are influenced by those experiences, relationships, and knowledge. And as I reflect on all I've accomplished, I want to share a final story that brings success into perspective.

LOSING MY MEDAL…& MY MIND

After winning at the Olympics and then graduating from college, I moved back to Hawaii to start my new life. My silver medal represented all of my life's labor, dedication and sacrifice. I was so concerned about someone breaking into our house and stealing it that I hid it where no burglar could find it. This became a problem when, after a few months, even I couldn't remember where I hid it. I tore up the whole house but still couldn't find it. I was discouraged, thinking I had lost the medal for good.

Embarrassed to admit my foolishness, I sheepishly went to my mom and confessed. In her loving way, she said, "You stupid kid!" Without a further word, she thought for a moment, then turned and walked to the dining room hutch. She pulled down a souvenir mug from the top shelf. I couldn't believe it. In thirty seconds she had found what I had given up as forever lost! (I will never understand how my mom and my wife have the uncanny ability to find lost items after I have searched the same places three times!)

MY GREATEST TREASURE REVEALED

How important was that medal to me? The silver medal represented the greatest achievement of my entire life's work; however, it is only a piece of metal. Over the years, it will tarnish and lose its shine. A thief could break in and steal it. When I'm long gone, it will be forgotten by the world. In fact, my name is only one line in the record books. My accomplishments have already become part of the past.

What good are all of my accomplishments and successes, if at the end of my life, I lose what is really important?

What if I achieve prestige in the world's eyes and lack approval from God? What if I get rich and enjoy every comfort that money can buy…but in the end lose my soul? Sure, success and accomplishments are wonderful. But in the light of eternity I believe that only one thing matters: **a personal relationship with Jesus Christ**.

Allow me to share with you how you can have a personal relationship with Christ. This has made all the difference in my life, and I would be remiss not to offer it to you.

YOUR GREATEST OPPORTUNITY

God created us with a purpose and destiny. Unless we discover His plan for our lives, we are never truly fulfilled. We try to satisfy our emptiness with things like money, accomplishments, pleasure, drugs, or relationships. These seem to satisfy, but are very temporary, never really bringing lasting or true contentment.

The basic problem is that we are sinners. The Bible says, "For **all** have sinned and fall short of the glory of God" (Romans 3:23). No matter how good we are, or how good our intentions are, we all do something wrong, and the Bible calls that "sin."

Because God is perfect and holy He cannot tolerate sin. Just as light and darkness cannot occupy the same room, a sinful person cannot stay in the presence of a holy God. The Bible goes on to say, "For the wages of sin is death" (Romans 6:23). This means all who have sinned – *all* of us – deserve death, or separation from God.

If God stopped there, our lives would be meaningless and without hope. Yet one of the most well-known verses in the Bible is also one of His greatest promises: John 3:16, which says, "For God so loved the world that He gave His one and only Son, that whoever believes in Him shall not perish but have eternal life." In other words, **God loved us so much that He provided a way to forgive our sins and give us eternal life.** God sent His Son, Jesus Christ, to die in our place. He lived a perfect life and, though He didn't have to, Jesus took the punishment for our sins. His death on the cross paved the way for us to escape punishment.

The exciting thing is that three days later, Jesus rose from the dead. This proved that He was not just a mortal man but indeed the Son of God. And by doing so He conquered sin and death to give us the free gift of eternal life.

Like any gift, though, we must receive it. How do we receive this greatest gift? <u>By believing in Jesus Christ</u>. That comes in three simple parts:

- First, admitting we are sinners who cannot save ourselves,
- Second, believing that Jesus died on the cross to forgive our sin,
- And finally, by committing our lives to follow Him.

When we do this, God will come into our hearts and change us.

"If you confess with your mouth, 'Jesus is Lord,' and believe in your heart that God raised Him from the dead, you will be saved" (Romans 10:9). There is nothing we can do to deserve God's love and forgiveness. We receive His promises free by faith.

YOUR INVITATION FROM GOD

When I heard about Jesus and what He had to offer, I knew I needed to have a personal relationship with Him. Deep in my heart I knew that nothing would satisfy my need for God. That evening I invited Jesus to come into my heart by saying a simple prayer. If you recognize that you need Jesus, then I invite you to say this simple prayer:

Dear Jesus, I admit that I am a sinner and cannot save myself. I believe that You died on the cross for me. Please forgive me for all of my sins. I invite You to come into my heart as my Lord and Savior. With Your strength I will live my life for You. In Jesus' name I pray, Amen.

If you sincerely prayed this prayer, God has forgiven you and has given you a new life with a new purpose. **You now have eternal life!**

When I received Jesus as my Lord, I didn't feel any different or experience any strong emotions. But in my heart I knew something had changed. From that time on, I attended a Bible-believing church and started to grow in faith. Accepting Jesus into my heart has been the best decision that I have ever made.

My prayer is that as you walk along your journey in life, you too will come to know Christ and have a personal relationship with Him. With Christ at the center of your life, He will give you hope and purpose that will change your life forever.

Afterword

Today I am a blessed man. I am married to Mari, the most wonderful woman in the world. She is my best friend, confidant, and lover. I can't imagine life without her. Next to my relationship with Christ, marrying her was the best decision of my life. I am also blessed with three beautiful daughters, Rena, Anna, and Maya. They are the joy of my life and when I hold them, I feel God's love and goodness. I never imagined how blessed I could be to have a loving family.

I've had diverse careers with a Fortune 500 company, a profitable small business, and a Christian church. Currently, I am a partner with Del Fujinaka of our own financial services company called Pacific Wealth Strategies LLC. As for judo, my body no longer moves as it used to, so I focus on using it to teach others how to live a life of success and significance.

My latest endeavor is a non-profit organization called Personal Transformation International (PTI) which I co-founded with my close friend and business partner Del Fujinaka. Our mission is to help every individual enter into a dominion of excellence and be personally transformed in the areas of finances, relationships, and well-being. It is through this personal transformation that each person will pursue their God given purpose with all their hearts. I believe that through this ministry we will impact many people around the world.

Through each new chapter, I continue to experience the joys of success and the pains of hardship and failure. Now more than ever, I am excited to run the journey that God has for me.

Won't you join me in living life to the fullest, just as God designed for us?

Acknowledgments

Who I am today is the result of the lives that have touched me through my life's journey. I have been blessed to have many people come into my life at the right time and give of themselves to help me grow and mature.

My parents **Henry and Karen**, my brother **Gary**, and my sister **Michelle** were the backbone of my support. They gave unselfishly, sacrificing so much to make my dreams their own. They shared in my victories and helped me through my defeats.

I have also had the privilege of learning under some of the most dedicated and caring head *sensei*: **Tsuruo Fukushima, Yotoku Maeshiro, Yasuyuki Sakabe, Warren Shimizu, Leigh Nakamoto, Larry Iwamuro, Reisuke Shiraishi, Albert Aoki, Nobuyuki Sato and Yosh Uchida**. I am deeply indebted to the many other instructors, teammates and competitors I worked out with and competed against throughout my eighteen-year competitive career.

Many thanks to the pastors who guided my spiritual walk: **Sam Webb, Elmer Inafuku, Emmanuel Cannistraci, Sidney Sumida, and Norman Nakanishi**.

Writing this book was a monumental team effort: Special thanks to my editors, **Dawn O'Brien and Elaine Terry**, who patiently went through my manuscript many times so that it could breathe life. Thank you, **Elizabeth Lyons**, for doing the final proofreading of the manuscript. Thanks to the many who also gave valuable input: **Henry Asano, Steve Bonior, Robert Brink, Dan Hatano, Norman Katayama, Al Kawamoto, Deron Kawamoto, Mike Mikasa, Leigh Nakamoto, Norman Nakanishi, Matthew Ogata, Russell Ogata, Herbert Shiraishi, Karen Shiratori, Frieda Takaki, Makoto Tanaka, Jimmy Yamada, Jr., Teruyoshi Yamaguchi** and **Cedric Yamanaka**. Thank you to **Dr. Danny Yamashiro** and **Dr. Daniel Kikawa** for the advice on writing, publishing, and distribution. A wonderful thank you to **Roy Kawaji** for providing inspiration and expertise through your personal and professional insight. **Michelle Liu**, thanks for helping with the synopsis on the back of the book and getting so excited when I told you I wanted to write a book! A wonderful thank you to **Del Fujinaka**. You have been a close friend and constant encouragement to me over the past several years in all the areas of my life.

A special thanks also to **Jimmy Yamada, Jr.**, who believed in me from the time when we first met. You encouraged me to never give up and have been a wonderful support to my judo, family, career, and vision.

Thanks to **David Finch**, for providing the photos that made this book come alive. Thank you to **White Mountain Castle Publishing, LLC** for helping me cross the finish line by publishing this book and making my story available to the world.

Finally, thank you to my wife, **Mari**. You are the love of my life and have shown your unconditional love and support for me. You have always loved me and believed in me, even when I doubted myself. Thank you for choosing me to be your husband and completing me.

Above all, I give glory to the **Lord Jesus Christ**. You are so good to me!

Kevin Asano's 18 year journey from humble beginnings training in his judo coach's garage in Pearl City, Hawaii to the pinnacle of sports success representing the United States at the 1988 Seoul Olympic games is filled with lessons and insights that will resonate with all of us. Against all odds, Asano earned the silver medal in judo at the Seoul Olympic Games. In 2000, he was inducted into the Hawaii Sports Hall of Fame and in 2002 into the San Jose State University Sports Hall of Fame. He is a 6th degree black belt and a professor of judo.

Asano is a partner in Pacific Wealth Strategies, LLC, a financial planning organization, and the co-founder of Personal Transformation International, a non-profit organization committed to transforming individuals by helping them find their life's calling.

Kevin and his wife, Mari, have three children and reside in Hawaii. He is a graduate of Pearl City High School and graduated with distinction from San Jose State University.

Kevin Asano
Email: info@stepontothemat.com
Internet: www.stepontothemat.com